WORLD WAR I
IN THE AIR

Peter Hepplewhite is an escaped history teacher, currently hiding in the Tyne and Wear Archives Service, where he works as Education Officer. He has been a freelance writer for more than ten years, starting with school textbooks (boo!) before he realized that war stories were more thrilling

Although David Wyatt is primarily known for his work on fiction, including novels by Terry Pratchett and Philip Pullman, he has a love of history and enjoys the education he receives when working on factual projects. He lives on Dartmoor, which is stuffed full of history, as well as amazing landscapes to stimulate his overactive imagination.

WORLD WAR I
IN THE AIR

PETER HEPPLEWHITE

Illustrations and maps by David Wyatt

MACMILLAN CHILDREN'S BOOKS

First published 2003 by Macmillan Children's Books
a division of Macmillan Publishers Limited
20 New Wharf Road, London N1 9RR
Basingstoke and Oxford
www.panmacmillan.com

Associated companies throughout the world

ISBN 0 330 41011 3

1 3 5 7 9 8 6 4 2

A CIP catalogue record for this book is available from
the British Library.

Typeset by Nigel Hazle
Printed and bound in Great Britain by Mackays of Chatham plc, Kent

CONTENTS

INTRODUCTION

A WORLD WAR

In August 1914 Europe went to war, with the Allies –
Britain, France and Russia taking on the Central Powers
– Germany and Austria-Hungary. Hopes of a short, sharp
conflict were soon dashed as the opposing armies dug in
on the Western Front – over 400 miles (600 km) of
trenches stretching from the Swiss border to the English
Channel. New and terrible weapons, especially artillery
and machine guns, brought a bloody stalemate and the
deaths of millions.

In four years of grim struggle, the war affected most
of the world. Troops from all over the Empire – India,
Canada, New Zealand and Australia – flocked to Britain's
aid, while Algerians and Africans fought alongside the
French. On the Eastern Front, after three years of hard
fighting, the Russian government collapsed and there was

a **communist revolution**.

In the war at sea, the Royal Navy rounded up or sank German raiders, and after the Battle of Jutland penned the enemy High Seas fleet into the Baltic. But enemy submarines, the sinister U-boats, were far harder to beat. Britain came close to starvation in 1917 because the U-boats sank so many ships carrying vital supplies of food.

The bloodshed was carried across the Alps when Italy declared war on the Allied side in 1915, while in the Middle East, Turkey joined the Germans. Soon British troops were battling the Turks in Mesopotamia (Iraq), Palestine, Arabia and the fatal, rocky shores of Gallipoli. In 1917 the USA joined the war, but it wasn't until the summer of 1918 that American soldiers arrived in large numbers in Europe. They came just in time to help the Allies break the last great German attack and turn defeat into victory.

War in the Air

Against this epic background a new type of combat was born – war in the air. But in August 1914 few could have guessed how momentous this would be. In Britain, the Royal Flying Corps (RFC) was a tiny branch of the army, with only 197 pilots and a few dozen planes. For most generals, aircraft were nothing more than a gimmick – at best, a cavalry patrol in the skies. Within months, however, aeroplanes had changed the face of warfare for ever.

Reconnaissance planes brought back vital information

about the movement of enemy troops and forced both sides to move their men and supplies by night. By 1915 aircraft equipped with radios could direct artillery fire, while intelligence officers pored over the details of the latest aerial photographs. Control of the skies became essential to victory and both sides developed ever more sophisticated fighting machines.

On 1 April 1918 the RFC became the Royal Air Force (RAF), Britain's third armed service and independent of the army. By this time the ramshackle squadrons of 1914 had been transformed. The RAF had more than 4,000 combat aircraft on the Western Front and 114,000 personnel. But the cost was high. In four years of fighting, Britain had trained a total of 22,000 pilots and more than half of these brave men were killed or injured. Civilians, too, were no longer secure behind the front lines. In a grim development, enemy airships and bombers had launched terror attacks into the heart of British cities.

This book highlights six stunning stories from the war in which aircraft came of age, and gives you the fighting facts behind them.

• *Cavalry in the Clouds*
In August 1914 the tiny RFC flies to France and finds itself in the path of a German knockout blow. But will anyone believe the pilots' reports of massive enemy troop movements?

• *A Strange Affair with a Machine Gun*

On 10 May 1915 Louis Strange is hanging from his plane by his fingertips – 8,000 feet (2,500 m) in the air. How did his obsession with machine guns lead to this predicament?

• *Airship Killer*

In 1915 German airships roam the skies over England. Are they really invulnerable to attack by aeroplanes or can they be stopped? One man is going to try ...

• *Gotha Summer*

In the summer of 1917 giant German bombers raid London and kill innocent civilians. Will the shock of these terror raids force the British to surrender?

• *Ace of Aces*

New pilot Edward 'Mick' Mannock seems boastful yet nervous. If he can overcome his flight nerves he has all the makings of a top-scoring ace. Will he be able to do it?

• *Sixty to One*

With the end of the war in sight, Canadian ace William Barker battles alone against a formation of 60 German planes. Can he possibly make it back home?

If your reading stalls or goes into a spin, help is at hand. Words shown in **bold** type are explained in RFC Lingo or the Glossary at the end of this book.

The performance of British aircraft is given in imperial measurements in these stories – the feet and miles per hour that the men of the RFC understood. You can convert them to metric measurements of speed and height using these tables.

Height

Feet	Metres
1,000	305
2,000	609
3,000	914
4,000	1,219
5,000	1,523
6,000	1,828
7,000	2,133
8,000	2,437
9,000	2,742
10,000	3,047
11,000	3,351
12,000	3,656
13,000	3,961
14,000	4,265
15,000	4,570
16,000	4,875
17,000	5,179
18,000	5,484
19,000	5,789
20,000	6,093
21,000	6,398

Speed

Miles per hour (mph)	Kilometres per hour (kph)
10	16
20	32
30	48
40	64
50	80
60	97
70	113
80	129
90	145
100	161
120	177
130	193
140	225
150	241

Song

We are the RFC
We cannot fight
We cannot shoot
What bloody use are we?
But when we reach Berlin
The Kaiser he will say
Mein Gott! Mein Gott!
What a jolly fine lot
Are the boys of the RFC.

Anon.

CAVALRY IN THE CLOUDS

BATTLE BRIEFING

Flying Fears

In 1903 Wilbur and Orville Wright made the first heavier-than-air flight at Kitty Hawk, North Carolina. For a feeble 12 seconds their plane skimmed across the sandy dunes. It hardly seemed a world-shaking event.

Yet within a few years the technology of flight had the British government worried. In 1908 a giant German airship flew 240 miles in 12 hours and the following year Frenchman Louis Blériot hopped from Calais to Dover in 37 minutes. Could it be that the Royal Navy and the Channel were no longer enough to make Britain safe from attack?

In 1912 the RFC was formed and the British finally began to take air power seriously. The main task of the RFC was to support the army, but there were few pilots and only a handful of planes. The service had to be built almost from scratch. It was ready, but only just, when Britain declared war on Germany on 4 August 1914.

The RFC wings proudly worn by British pilots

No one, least of all the generals, believed planes made from wood and fabric could be effective weapons. Their job was not to attack enemy troops – it was reconnaissance. Pilots were expected to be little more than aerial taxi drivers – the important men in the sky were the observers. What the army wanted from the RFC was the chance to spy out enemy troop movements, gun positions and defences – a job previously done by cavalry patrols. Soon, however, airmen would stop waving when they passed an enemy plane and start shooting.

OFF TO FRANCE

On 9 August 1914 the British Expeditionary Force (BEF)

– 80,000 men, 30,000 horses and 315 field guns – began their embarkation for France. With transports leaving every 10 minutes from Portsmouth and Southampton, the Channel seemed choked with ships. This has been called 'the best army ever to leave Britain' – highly trained and well equipped. When they landed, the smiling soldiers were given a heroes' welcome. But such good times would be short-lived. Already, complex war plans were unfolding.

The French had launched their main attack against Germany in Alsace-Lorraine. They believed their fighting spirit would soon break the enemy and sweep them on to Berlin. To support France, the British agreed to take up a covering position just inside the border of Belgium. It was a fateful move. The BEF marched smack into the path of a mighty German right hook – an army of 750,000 smashing through Belgium to encircle the French and bring the war to a rapid end.

In the face of this hammer blow, what possible use would a few dozen underpowered aeroplanes be? The army was about to find out ...

Learning the Lessons of War

Following hard on the heels of the BEF, the infant RFC prepared to go into battle. And like the British Army, it faced an impressive enemy. The Germans had 246 planes and seven airships, by far the largest air force of the European powers. Against this the RFC was tiny, with

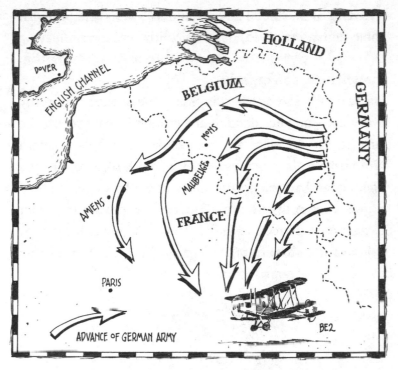

The dramatic German advance through Belgium, 1914

only four fully operational squadrons – 48 planes. But if enthusiasm counted, they would make their mark!

The journey to France was organized in a madcap hurry. First, the planes were to fly from their home airfields and gather at Dover, then they would cross the Channel in an aerial flotilla – the biggest flight of aircraft ever seen in Britain. And what a mixed bunch they were: 2 and 4 Squadrons were equipped with the BE2 – the best plane at the time – but the others were a jumble of Blériots, Henri Farmans, Avros and Sopwith Tabloids (see page 25).

Eyewitness to Tragedy

Gathering a force like this was a new experience for everyone – and accidents were waiting to happen. On 12 August, as 3 Squadron prepared to take off from Netherhaven, a grumpy air mechanic looked on. James McCudden had joined the army as a boy bugler before transferring to the RFC in 1913. He was desperately keen to become a pilot and eager for any flying he could get.

James had been promised a lift in a two-seater

James McCudden, 1914

machine to Dover, but at the last minute his pilot had been ordered to take a single-seat plane. Now all he could do was look on dourly as the others had all the fun. He swung the prop for Lieutenant Robert Skene and his passenger, Air Mechanic Keith Barlow, and ducked under the wing to pull away the chocks. Skene trundled across the airfield and took off, disappearing behind one of the hangars. Then – SILENCE – the engine stopped. After what seemed an age James heard a noise like a distant clap of thunder.

He wrote later:

I ran for half a mile, and found the machine in a small copse of firs, so I got over the fence and pulled the wreckage away from the occupants and found them both dead ... I shall never forget that morning at about half past six, kneeling by poor Keith Barlow and looking at the rising sun and then again at poor Barlow, who had no superficial injury and was killed purely by concussion, and wondering if it was going to be like this always.

James couldn't know the heartbreaking answer that August dawn would be 'yes'.

James McCudden became an air ace with **57 kills** to his credit. Sadly, in 1918, three months after he was awarded the Victoria Cross, he died in an accident – when his engine stalled after take-off.

To France

On 13 August 1914 the British squadrons hopped across the Channel from Dover. The aircrew carried inflated car-tyre inner tubes to act as lifebelts if they ditched in the sea. Luckily nobody took the plunge, but one flyer impishly tried to drop his inner tube, like a fairground hoop, on to the top of the lighthouse at Cap Gris-Nez. After a 2-hour flight the British landed at Amiens. The first man on French soil was the high-spirited Lieutenant Hubert Harvey-Kelly. Just how high-spirited you'll find out shortly.

Following the aircraft as quickly as possible, the ground staff crossed to France in steam ships. The stores and heavy goods were loaded in a motley collection of civilian vehicles **commandeered** by the army –

Hubert Harvey-Kelly (on right) with a BE2a reconnaissance plane, August 1914

delivery lorries emblazoned with such slogans as LAZENBY'S SAUCE (THE WORLD'S APPETIZER), PEEK FREAN'S BISCUITS and STEPHENS' BLUE-BLACK INK. There was even a large van with the word BOVRIL painted in bold, black letters on it. Along the way the French people turned out to welcome the RFC. Air Mechanic James Gascoyne remembered:

> They assembled along the road and gave us terrific cheers and we were loaded up with wine, bottles of wine everywhere – the lorries had more wine than equipment I think! As a result I've never drunk wine since.

In the Path of the Hammer Blow

From their forward base at Maubeuge, the British aircraft were soon at work, spotting the movement of German troops. The first report, made on 19 August, was disappointing. If it had been the observer's homework, it would have scored 0/10!

> Did not pick my position on the map. Arrived at a big town, but could not place it on the map. On my return I discovered this to have been Brussels.

Thankfully the quality improved quickly. On 22 August machine after machine returned with alarming sightings of a vast enemy attack. Lieutenant Charles Rabagliati reported:

As soon as we got over our area, instead of seeing a few odd Germans I saw the whole area covered with hordes of field grey uniforms – advancing infantry, cavalry, transport and guns. In fact it looked as though the whole place was alive with Germans.

The sea of grey spotted by the awed lieutenant was the powerful German II Corps, which was about to slam into the BEF. The enemy had caught the British by surprise – and outnumbered them three to one. For a long, hard day the BEF held the Germans back in bitter street-fighting in the mining town of Mons. But the odds were so stacked against them that if the British did not retreat quickly they would be annihilated.

Retreat

On the evening of 23 August the British commander, Sir John French, weighed up the disturbing news given to him by the RFC. He didn't like it. In fact Sir John was one of those generals who wondered if aeroplanes weren't a new-fangled waste of time. But as report after report came in confirming the huge size of the German force, he decided to act. He cancelled plans for a counter-attack and ordered the BEF to pull out. He made the painful decision just in time.

In the blazing August heat, the BEF made a gallant fighting retreat – not knowing when or where it would end. The RFC abandoned their airfield at Maubeuge as

German shells pounded the site. Fuel and stores were set on fire, even as the planes took to the air. The ground crew piled into the lorries with essential equipment and set off down roads packed with soldiers and refugees.

Day after day the RFC pulled back with the army, flying from makeshift landing strips in fields of corn or, worse still, rutted fields of cabbages. This took a heavy toll on the delicate aircraft, with mechanics working though the night to repair shattered landing gear. Sometimes the ground crew had to pack up and run while the planes were in the air. Exhausted pilots returned from missions only to play a frustrating game of 'hunt the base'. One marker became a good luck symbol. The faithful Bovril lorry, with its large black letters, was unmistakable from the air.

Curious Combat

With ferocious fighting on the ground, it wasn't long before the airmen decided to join in. Pilots from both sides carried pistols, rifles and grenades, but during those first days of the war had done little more than annoy each other with them. On 25 August, however, two incidents showed that the conflict in the air was heating up too. The first was quite light-hearted.

Three BE2s from 2 Squadron were on patrol when they spotted a German Taube observing the French battle lines. The Taube, which means 'dove' in German, was a strange-looking plane, with wings shaped like those of a bird. It made a tempting target. Flight leader Lieutenant Hubert Harvey-Kelly dived into the attack. (Remember Hubert was described as 'high-spirited' – how about adding 'as mad as a hatter'!)

The bird-like Taube, designed by Austrian Igo Etrich

Determined to scare the life out of the enemy pilot, he brought the thrashing propeller of his BE2 to within 4 feet (1.25 m) of the tail of his victim. One small mistake and both planes would be spinning towards the hard earth. Joining in the sport, the other British pilots closed in on either side, while Hubert hung on behind.

The wretched German cursed the **Tommies** and tried to throw them off, but they stuck like glue. Worse, he could see they were cackling with laughter. Desperately, he landed in the nearest field and heaved a sigh of relief. Safe! Or maybe not ... He glanced round to find the crazy

British landing beside him. Were they about to kill him?

Not surprisingly, he didn't wait to find out. Leaping from his plane, the German pilot sprinted towards nearby woods to hide. Imagine his horror when Hubert and the others noisily chased him, prowling through the undergrowth. After a few minutes' fruitless search, they gave up, set fire to the Taube and took off, leaving behind one very relieved enemy flyer.

Although this reads like a storyboard for an early Charlie Chaplin movie, it set a war record – the first victory in the air. And so far no one had been harmed. The second incident on that summer's day was far less innocent.

Lieutenant Rabagliati was patrolling at around 3–4,000 feet (925 1,230 m) when he came across a German plane. Both crews began to take potshots, Rabagliati with his Lee Enfield rifle, the German observer with a Mauser pistol, and neither pilot backed down. The lieutenant wrote later:

> We manoeuvred ourselves against one another. Sometimes we'd be extremely close, it seemed almost touching, other times we'd be out of range. We couldn't shoot through the propeller in front so we shot sideways. Not only was the other aeroplane going fast, but our own from which I was shooting was going fast. We fired a great many rounds – I fired over 100 – and then suddenly … I saw the German pilot fall forward on to his joystick and the machine tipped and went down.

There was nothing of the silent film comedy in this encounter. A long war of kill or be killed had just begun in the air.

In those crazy August days the RFC came through its baptism of fire proudly. Like the soldiers they flew over, the airmen fell back in good order, leapfrogging from one makeshift airfield to another but always patrolling and reporting enemy movements. Crucially, British generals now had no doubts as to how useful the RFC had become. The early warning given to Sir John French had helped to save the BEF from extinction. And soon the time would come to turn and fight again ...

FIGHTING FACTS

What Happened to the BEF?

The retreat from Mons is a proud episode in the history of the British Army. For 14 days the BEF made a fighting retreat and didn't break. It was tiny by European standards, but the soldiers were professionals. They could fire 15 rounds a minute from their Lee Enfield rifles and made the German **conscripts** pay a heavy price.

Finally the running came to an end on the River Marne and, together with the French, the BEF turned to launch a counter-attack. Now the Germans were driven back and both sides began a race to the sea in an effort to outflank each other. By October the rival armies had dug lines of trenches that stretched from the English Channel to Switzerland. This was the Western Front. Over the next four years the tiny British Army of 1914 grew to a force of over 4 million, able to slug it out with the Germans on equal terms. And as the army grew so did the RFC, from the few dozen planes of August 1914 to 22,647 aeroplanes and seaplanes by November 1918.

Gentlemen Only

So you reckon you are pilot material? Think you've got what it takes? Well, in 1914 your selection interview for the RFC might have gone something like this:

'How do you do? Take a seat. Right, Mr ... Can you ride a horse? sail a boat? ride a motorcycle?

'Yes? Well done, you are just the type we want. With the skills you've learned from these sports – coordination, steady nerve, sense of balance – we'll have you flying solo in two hours.

'Now try this eyesight test. Can you pick out the different colours in this bundle of woollen strands? Red? Excellent! Green? Fine! Yellow? Marvellous!

'By the way, one last question, old chap. What's your background? Family and all that? Your father's a plumber? Oh dear! Sorry. Perhaps there might be a place for you in the infantry. We have standards to keep up, you know.'

In 1914 flying with the RFC was like becoming a member of an exclusive club for gentlemen. Most early recruits came from privileged backgrounds. One reason for this was money. Candidates were expected to pass the Royal Aero Club certificate of competence at their own expense, before they joined up. And this cost £70, at a time when a good wage for an ordinary worker was £3 a week.

By 1916 the supply of young men from public schools like Eton had begun to dry up. Reluctantly the RFC allowed working-class candidates like James McCudden and Edward 'Mick' Mannock (see pages 12–13) to train as pilots. Even so, older hands didn't like it and commented that the service had become 'quite a mixed bunch'. This wasn't meant as a compliment.

James McCudden

Earlier in this chapter you met James McCudden as a disgruntled air mechanic. For much of his career he was to stay disgruntled with the RFC and he became an **ace** the hard way. Repeated applications to become a pilot were turned down, but he was determined to gain experience. In 1915 he flew as an observer, fitting in the flying between his normal ground duties. In 1916 he was finally sent for pilot training and gained his 'wings' – his first-class pilot's certificate – on 30 May. He made his first kill on 6 September, bringing down a two-seater Albatros. By April 1918, when he was awarded the VC, he had shot down 54 enemy planes. The long citation commended his exceptional skill, noting:

> On two occasions, he totally destroyed four two-seater enemy aeroplanes on the same day, and on the last occasion all four machines were destroyed in the space of one hour and 30 minutes.

James added another three to his score before he was killed when his aircraft stalled after take-off on 9 July.

For more on aces turn to page 96.

Primitive Planes

To modern eyes the aircraft of 1914 look incredibly fragile.

- **Structure:** Most of the main parts were made from wood such as ash and spruce, braced with steel wires.
- **Skin:** The outer covering was made from fabric, often the finest Irish linen painted with acetone dope (varnish) to pull it taut and give it a smooth surface.
- **Cockpit:** The pilot sat on a seat made of wicker, often on top of the fuel tank. The RFC refused to fit armour plate to protect pilots from ground fire, even though the Germans soon began to do this.
- **Engines:** Most early British planes were powered by French rotary engines in which the cylinders whirled around a stationary shaft. Few aircraft had brakes. On the ground aeroplanes were held back by crewmen until the engine had built up enough revs for take-off.

- *Performance:* The average speed was about 60 mph (100 kph), with maximum heights ranging between 3,300 feet and 12,000 feet (950 and 3,500 m). While flight duration was good – most planes could stay in the air for 2 to 4 hours – the loads they could carry were still small. Even the weight of the pilot was crucial!

Don't Shoot! We're British!

One of the biggest problems facing RFC aircrew was the hail of rifle and machine-gun fire from the ground. Worse, it often came from BOTH sides. British soldiers were under orders not to shoot at aircraft unless they were certain they were German, but in practice they blazed away at anything that flew within range. The answer seemed to be clear: put markings on RFC planes – something that said, 'HOLD ON, WE'RE ON YOUR SIDE!' The enemy had already done this. The underside of every German aircraft was painted white with a large black cross on each wing.

At first the British tried painting their planes with a Union Jack, but this just looked like a smudge from the ground. The next idea was far more successful – the red, white and blue roundels still used by the RAF today. Although pilots nicknamed these 'the targets', fewer aircraft were shot down once they were given the new symbols.

Aircraft in the RFC, 1914

Type and country of origin	Crew and purpose	Speed	Weapons	Comments
Farman Longhorn – France	2 Reconnaissance & training	59 mph (94 kph) at sea level	None	Successful in its day. Flew a record distance of 350 miles (560 km) in 1910
Blériot XI – France	1 or 2 Reconnaissance	66 mph (105 km) at sea level	None	The RFC had 23 of these machines when the war began
BE2a – Britain	2 Reconnaissance	72 mph (115 kph) at 6,500 feet (2,000 m)	None at first, but the BE2c was armed with a **Lewis gun** by 1915	Designed by Geoffrey de Havilland, the BE2 was the first British aircraft to arrive in France
Avro 504 – Britain	2 Trainer	84 mph (134 kph) at sea level	None, but some were later fitted with Lewis guns for home-defence against Zeppelins or Gothas	Over 8,000 were made during the war, largely used to train pilots
Sopwith Tabloid – Britain	1 High-speed reconnaissance	$92^1/2$ mph (148 kph) at sea level	Usually none	Fitted with bomb racks by the Royal Naval Air Service, two Tabloids bombed Zeppelin sheds in October 1914

Aye-Aye! What's This?

Throughout the war reconnaissance remained the most important task of the RFC. The big battles would be won or lost on the ground and the generals needed all the information they could get. Only aircraft could probe beyond the German lines.

At first most observers were army officers, hastily scribbling notes or marking new features on maps. But the naked eye had its limitations. Sometimes it was difficult to notice small changes, such as a new machine-gun positions on a complex system of enemy trenches. Yet such tiny details could be crucial during an attack. What the army needed was a means of checking changes over time – in other words, they needed photographs!

A War of Lenses

The first British photos were taken during the Battle of the Aisne in 1915, using big, clumsy and heavy box cameras. The shots were taken though a hole cut in the floor of the plane. The problems were recalled by Lieutenant Archibald:

> *You yelled at the pilot when you were going to take a photograph so he kept the aircraft quite level and didn't tilt the angle of the camera ... It was a difficult job, because first you had to look through the hole to see the target you were photographing. Then you lost sight of it as you put the camera between your knees and pressed the trigger. I became rather the star photographer, being very small and able to bend down to adjust the camera.*

By 1916 techniques had improved so much that a picture taken from 15,000 feet (4,500 m) could be magnified to show the footprints of an infantryman. In the last two years of the war the British alone took more than half a million reconnaissance photos.

The Dying Aviator

This song, with its black humour, soon
became an RFC favourite

A handsome young airman lay dying
Lay dying. (Chorus)
And as on the aerodrome he lay.
He lay.
To the mechanics who came round him
   sighing.
Came sighing.
These last dying words he did say.
He did say.
'Take the cylinder out of my kidneys.
Of his kidneys.
The connecting rod out of my brain.
Of his brain.
From the small of my back take the camshaft
His back
And assemble the engine again.'

                                (Again.)

                                   Anon.

A STRANGE
AFFAIR WITH
A MACHINE
GUN

BATTLE BRIEFING

By the end of November 1914 the war on the ground had reached stalemate. As the troops dug in, generals on both sides looked to their air forces to give them an edge. Britain rushed ahead with plans to expand the RFC, training more pilots and observers, and also the small army of men needed to keep them in the air – armourers, fitters, mechanics and riggers. By May 1915 2,260 new aircraft were on order.

Ideas about war in the air were changing quickly too. In August 1914 RFC Staff Officer Sykes had said, 'There should be no attempt at aerial conflict', and the Germans agreed with him. Yet by the spring of 1915 both sides had developed 'scouts' – fighting aircraft designed to shoot down enemy planes and protect their own reconnaissance flights.

Ominously, these scouts were armed not just with rifles or pistols – they carried machine guns.

On the British side, one of the pioneers of this lethal technology was Lieutenant Louis Strange. In 1915 he was to experience one of the most bizarre episodes of the war.

AERIAL ATHLETICS

A Horse of Course

Louis was a Dorset farmer and a very good horseman. He was never happier than when out with the local hunt. Nothing could beat a good gallop across the countryside: the cry of the hounds, the charging horsemen, the joy of the chase. It was a wonderful English tradition that sorted the men from the boys!

One exhilarating chase found him in the saddle for an hour and 40 minutes. Flushed with excitement, he leapt every barrier in his path – gates, hedges and ditches flying by. At the end he was the only rider still up with the hounds. For a countryman, it was a memory to treasure.

Horses were Louis's greatest love – until he saw his first aeroplane at the army **manoeuvres** in September 1912. Like many keen horsemen, Louis was a part-time soldier in the Dorset Yeomanry – a unit of volunteer cavalry. The Dorset troopers attended the manoeuvres every year to sharpen their skills, but that September there was a novelty: the newly formed RFC joined in too.

Learning New Lessons

As the planes buzzed and wheeled overhead, most soldiers dismissed them as thrilling but useless toys. What good were they compared to a dashing troop of cavalry? But Louis wasn't so sure ...

In the manoeuvres, the army divided into two teams, each led by a general determined to outfox his opponent. Sir James Grierson, the commander of Blue Team, was up against Sir Douglas Haig, the leader of Red Team. Each side was supported by seven RFC aeroplanes and an airship. In the opinion of most, Grierson was the underdog – a plodder – but on the day he made better use of his flyers.

As each side took position, one of Blue Team's planes spotted Red troops deploying for a mass attack. At once the crew flew back to HQ to report, only to find Grierson downcast by their news. He had already sent his cavalry in the wrong direction – the war games were lost before the fighting had begun. At once the airmen stepped into the breach. They flew new orders to the Blue cavalry, who neatly turned round and chopped off the Red advance. Grierson realized he had glimpsed the future.

*

The impression left on my mind is that their use has revolutionized the art of war. So long as hostile aircraft are hovering over one's troops all movements are liable to be seen and reported, and therefore the first step in war will be to get rid of the hostile aircraft.

Sadly, Grierson's opinions were ignored and the same lessons had to be learned again in 1914–15.

Back in Dorset, the yeomanry had long and loud arguments as the beer flowed after training sessions. Most troopers stayed faithful to the horse. In the next war, they argued, cavalry would be the decisive weapon. What could beat the massed charge of horses and the cold steel of the sabre?

But Louis knew that times were changing. He agreed with Grierson. 'Since that Blériot chap flew the Channel without falling into it, Britain is no longer an island,' he declared. 'Mark my words, within a few years aeroplanes will replace cavalry.'

As glasses were drained, and drained again, Louis issued his challenge. He would learn to fly . . . and what's more he would swoop over the Dorset Yeomanry at the manoeuvres in 1914. The bet was eagerly taken on all sides.

Flight School
Louis joined the RFC in 1913 and took his first lessons at the new Central Flying School at Upavon Downs on Salisbury Plain. The aeroplanes and the flight instructors

were a motley collection of men and machines, mostly brought in from France.

One instructor, Louis Noel, always gave a blunt speech to his perky pupils before their first solo flight:

I have told you how to fly. Have you understood? Yes? Well, I give you the last chance to say no ... Very well, you can fly, do you hear? I, Louis Noel, say you can fly. I speak no more. I go to the bar. If you commit suicide that is bad, but if you almost do that it will be much the worse for you.

Noel went on to become a French ace.

Fortunately, it was quite hard to be killed in the underpowered and slow machines of the time. They were little more than powered gliders with large areas of canvas and wood to absorb the shock of a crash. For new pupils, flying was limited to early mornings or late evenings – or other times when there was little wind. A training aircraft usually had no cockpit, just a seat for the instructor and a perch behind his back for the trainee.

Louis later recalled his early lessons with some amusement:

We knew nothing of the dual-control method of instruction. The pupil sat behind the instructor and could reach over his shoulder and use the control stick. There was, however, no way for the pupil to get his legs into contact with the rudder bar.

33

A student and instructor in a biplane

After a few lessons instructor and pupil changed places. Louis earned his pilot's licence in three weeks without any accidents.

With a Machine Gun to France

Louis went on to become a proficient flyer and was assigned as a lieutenant to 5 Squadron. On 1 May 1914 he took part in a daring new RFC training exercise – a bomb-dropping competition. Already a few flyers believed their planes could join in rather than just observe the fighting on the ground. From 300 feet (90 m) Louis's tiny bombs landed in a spread that averaged only $25\frac{1}{4}$ feet (8 m) from the centre of the target. Remarkable! It was close enough to win the competition, but not to impress watching army officers.

Planes carrying bombs? A waste of time, they argued. Yes, some aircraft hit the target, but conditions were perfect. What would happen if they were being shot at? What about bad weather? And look at the payload – so small as to be worthless.

When the war began, the RFC was still under strict orders to observe and report, not to fight. Louis, however, wasn't put off. He already had another bee in his bonnet: he wanted to fit a machine gun in his plane.

It sounded a preposterous idea. A gun and ammunition would be a heavy load, perhaps too heavy. The recoil (the kickback when the gun was fired) meant the weapon had to be fastened to the aircraft structure or it would fly out of the hands of the gunner. More difficult still, it had to be fired through the web of struts and wires that held the plane together. There was a running joke among pilots that not even a bird could fly through this maze. So what chance of blasting away with a stream of bullets without bringing the whole blooming thing down? But Louis was determined. While his **CO** turned a quizzical blind eye, he strapped a Lewis gun to his aircraft, a Maurice Farman 'Loghorn'.

Louis had little time to practise with his new weapon before war broke out. And more annoying still, when the RFC flew to France (see page 14) he was left behind. For three days irritating delays left him hopping with frustration on the ground. And then he was lumbered with a passenger who turned the cross-Channel flight

The Maurice Farman S7 Longhorn

into a mini-adventure. The man, a transport driver, was drunk – and heavy.

When Louis finally took off for Amiens on 16 August his underpowered plane was ridiculously full. The groaning Farman carried:

- pilot . . . and full kit
- 13-stone (83 kg) passenger . . . and full kit
- machine gun . . . and ammunition.

The aircraft **cut daisies** for a long time before it finally clawed into the air. After a $2^1/2$-hour flight through torrential rain, Louis landed, and his plane was surrounded by a cheering French crowd. Graciously, and unsteadily, the transport driver stood up and waved back – with an empty whisky bottle.

Too Slow

On 22 August, just before the enemy sledgehammer hit the BEF, a cheeky German flyer in an Albatros biplane decided to tweak the nose of the RFC. And it worked. As he flew 4,000 feet (1,230 m) over their airfield at Maubeuge the intruder stirred up a hornet's nest. Outraged British pilots grabbed an assortment of rifles, pistols and hand grenades and ran to their planes. If they could catch 'the **Hun**' they intended to bring him down.

Louis set off as eagerly as the rest. Was this the day the machine gun would prove its worth? Well, no. He soon lagged far behind the others, the weight of the gun proving too much for the Farman in a climb. He wrote:

> I set off with Lt. Penn Gaskell to work the Lewis gun. The enemy machine made off while we were still climbing over our aerodrome, and I imagine its occupants must have enjoyed a good laugh at our futile efforts.

But bad news was in store when he landed. Louis's CO ordered him to unship the gun and its mounting and make do with a rifle. Then at least he might be able to catch the enemy sometimes.

Getting Rid of Hostile Aircraft

In the following months Sir James Grierson's 1912 prediction came true. A few enterprising pilots took the lead in equipping their aircraft to enable them to shoot down German planes. If the skies were cleared of enemy reconnaissance flights, they argued, the German Army would be blinded.

As the action hotted up, Louis complained long and loud about his impounded machine gun. His mission reports summed up the problem. On 15 October, flying a two-man Avro, he chased and caught an enemy Aviatik. His observer blasted away with a rifle, but the chances of doing any damage while firing in an 80-mph (130 kph) slipstream were slim. Over 70 bullets later, with no hits, they saw the German duck into a cloud and escape, unharmed.

Finally Louis won his argument and was allowed to experiment with a machine gun again. The Avro was a **tractor** plane, not a pusher like the Farman. This meant the propeller was in the way, so the Lewis gun could fire only sideways and behind. Even so, it soon paid off. On 22 November, as Louis was returning to base, he spotted another Aviatik. This time he had the advantage of height and dived to attack.

As they zoomed across the bows of the enemy plane, Louis's observer, Lieutenant Small, let fly with a broadside and then another long burst as Louis closed in again. The German pilot **put on rudder** and slipped to one side, letting his observer, a Prussian guard officer, return fire with a pistol. Then ... CLACK, CLACK ... CLACK ... the Lewis gun was empty. Great timing!

Hastily – which wasn't all that hasty, with hands encumbered by thick flying gloves – Lieutenant Small changed the **drum** and opened fire again. Immediately the Aviatik fell away on one wing as the pilot dived steeply to escape. Around 20 machine-gun bullets had just peppered the instrument panel inches in front of his face. He wanted out and was almost over German lines and safe. But Louis was in no mood to let him go. He followed the Aviatik down and cut in front of it, less than 1,500 feet (460 m) from the enemy's trenches. At that moment a plume of black smoke came from the Aviatik's engine and the plane lumbered down to land in a field in the British reserve lines.

Machine-gun Athletics

Louis was at the start of a lethal race. By the summer of 1915 French, Germans and British were all flying fighter aircraft fitted with machine guns. But the technology was still unreliable – as he was about to find out.

Louis now joined 6 Squadron as flight leader and, because of his experience, had the pick of a mixed bag of aircraft. His choice was the first single-seat, tractor biplane assigned to the unit, a Martinsyde Scout. As planes went, it had all the flying ability of a pig. It was slow, unstable and sluggish in responding to the controls. What it did have, though, was a Lewis gun fitted to a fixed mounting on top of the upper wing – so it fired over the propeller. Louis was happy.

On 10 May he was on patrol behind German lines when he caught sight of an Aviatik well above him. At a painful 60 mph (100 kph), the best the Martinsyde could do, he climbed in pursuit. So far so good, until the enemy observer glanced down and warned the pilot that a British plane was closing in. Now a race was on and the Aviatik slowly began to pull away.

At around 8,500 feet (2,600 m) the Martinsyde reached its **ceiling** and Louis knew his prey would be out of reach in seconds. Pulling the **joystick** back to lift the nose, he fired a long burst that emptied the Lewis gun. And missed. Cursing, he watched the Aviatik fly peacefully on – undamaged.

When Louis calmed down he began to realize he was in a risky position. He'd flown a long way into enemy skies and the defenceless Martinsyde made a tempting target. Time to turn for home. Time to change the ammo drum. Time for the most terrifying moments of his life . . .

Louis's thoughts ran at lightning speed: 'The Lewis gun is on top of the upper wing . . . Hold the joystick between knees . . . Stretch up to unclip the drum. One quick twist and . . . Damn . . . Stuck. Assess situation: in a gentle dive back to Allied lines . . . about 20 miles away . . . Air speed about 75 mph. OK. Try again. Gloves off for a better grip. Stand up this time . . . Good grasp . . . HEAVE . . . HEAVE. Oh no! Plane's almost at stalling speed . . . Port wing has dropped . . . Losing balance . . . Fallen against joystick . . . Full left rudder . . . Going into a spin . . . Safety belt has come loose . . . Hold on!'

To Louis's horror, the plane rolled over and pointed its undercarriage at the sky. He was left dangling underneath, like a circus trapeze artist, but here there was no safety net. All that stopped him plummeting to earth was his vice-like grip on the ammo drum. And all that stopped the drum coming loose was a 6-mm crossed thread of low-tensile steel.

Louis wrote later:

Only a few seconds before I had been cursing because I could not get the drum off. Now I prayed fervently that it would stay on for ever.

If the drum came loose he was dead.

Louis Strange dangling upside down from his plane

For how long could you hold your weight, hanging from a bar in a gym? For how long could you hold on to a slowly spinning, upside-down biplane? A spin that was making you sick with dizziness?

Exactly! Now think about Louis's plight for a head-spinning second!

Louis knew he had to act fast. Letting go with one hand, he reached back and made a blind grab for a wing strut. This left him hanging momentarily from the drum by one hand. (Now try that in the gym!) Once he had a good grip on the strut, he began a series of swinging kicks to lever his legs into the cockpit. On the third attempt he hooked one foot in, then the other, booted the joystick to **jam on full aileron and rudder**. . . and flopped into the cockpit as the Martinsyde righted itself.

Danger Over? No!

The plane was in a roaring dive towards the Belgian town of Menin and had fallen almost 7,000 feet (2,150 m). Struggling against gravity, Louis managed to push his feet on to the rudder controls, correct the spin and level out.

Shaken to the core, he flew back to base – and sheepishly stayed quiet about the incident. He didn't want to be a laughing stock for weeks. This had two weird results.

- *Weird result one*: He was put on a charge by his commanding officer for damaging his seat and instruments by kicking them. Unfair or what?

- **Weird result two**: The crew of the German Avaitik claimed a victory. They had *seen* the British plane turn over and the pilot fall out. But there was no wreckage to back their claim . . . and no one would believe their story.

FIGHTING FACTS

'Let Me Report Him'

Remember the Aviatik brought down by Louis on 22 November 1914? The British infantrymen who captured the German flyers passed on a hilarious tale.

- The pilot had landed because he was terrified. But, although the engine was damaged, it would have made it back to German lines.
- The Prussian officer/observer thought they had landed because the pilot was injured. He was furious when he found out what had really happened.
- The Prussian threw aside the British soldiers and started to beat up the pilot. When he was held back he cried out in anguish: 'Let me report this coward to German flying headquarters.'

The Race for the Machine Gun

In spite of the efforts of British pilots like Louis, it was the French who led the way in air warfare. On 5

October 1914 an observer called Louis Quenault shot down an Aviatik with a Hotchkiss machine gun. The French plane was a rear-engined Voisin so, unlike in Louis's two-man Avro, mounting a machine gun that could fire forward wasn't a problem. By February 1915 the French had around 50 pushers equipped with similar guns.

But a far more important breakthrough was already being tested. In December 1914 the French pilot Roland Garros visited the workshops of plane builder Raymond Saulnier. Roland was a famous stunt flyer before the war, setting a world record for high flying of an astonishing 18,000 feet (5,500 m). He came to Raymond with a complaint. So far, he had been unable to shoot down any Germans:

When I was able to outmanoeuvre my adversary, my observer never succeeded in shooting him down with a light rifle.

What he wanted was a device that would allow him to fire a fixed, forward-mounted machine gun through his own whirling airscrew and not blast off the propeller blades. This meant that as he manoeuvred his plane, he also aimed his own weapon. Could Saulnier suggest an answer? Working together, the two men came up with a simple solution: deflector plates. They worked out that only about 7 per cent of the bullets would hit the propeller blades, so why not bounce them out of the way?

Sounds like a crazy idea? It was. If the bullets bounced off the plates in the wrong direction, the pilot could shoot down his own plane. But, although it was crude, it worked. Roland used his own Morane monoplane for the experiments and in April 1915 brought down five enemy planes in two weeks. That summer Allied pilots in Moranes fitted with deflector plates ruled the sky – but theirs was a short-lived joy.

Fokker Fodder

On 18 April Roland was flying low over German lines – too low – when a single bullet fired from the ground cut his fuel line. The engine died and he had no choice but to land behind enemy lines. Desperately, he tried to burn the Morane to protect its secrets, but he was too slow. Troops arrived and captured the precious plane. Roland was heartbroken – he had helped to develop a battle-winning weapon, only to hand it over to the Germans.

They, of course, were jubilant. So this was the mystery plane that was doing so much damage! The Morane was dismantled and the gun, engine and propeller were given to Anthony Fokker, a brilliant Dutch aircraft designer working in Germany. And with them came a personal message from the head of the German air force, Oberstleutnant Hermann von der Lieth-Thomsen: could he produce a forward-firing machine gun as good or better than this?

Remarkably, Fokker's team came up with an answer in

a few days. They had already designed a monoplane scout similar to the Morane – the Fokker E1. Made of welded steel tubes instead of wood, it was light and fast. Now they armed it with the first synchronized machine gun. Instead of the propeller stopping the bullets, it was connected to the gun by a pushrod control mechanism. When the trigger was pressed an even spread of bullets flew between the blades without striking them.

Improved Fokker Ells were delivered to German frontline units during the summer of 1915. The plane was to make two fearsome aces: Oswald Boelcke and Max Immelman. By early 1916 Allied pilots felt they were little more than 'Fokker fodder'. Even RFC HQ seemed to be admitting defeat when it issued a rather desperate order:

The Fokker El, 1915

Until the Royal Flying Corps are in possession of a machine as good or better than the German Fokker ... it must be laid down as a hard and fast rule that a machine proceeding on reconnaissance must be escorted by at least three fighting machines.

Fokker Foiled

In 1916 the MP Pemberton Billing caused an outrage in the House of Commons when he deplored the poor quality of British aircraft:

Every one of our pilots at the front knows when he steps into them that if he gets back it will be more by luck and his skill than any mechanical assistance that he will get from the people who provide him with the machines ... I would suggest that quite a number of officers in the RFC have been murdered rather than killed.

Strong stuff. But even as he spoke a new generation of aircraft was tipping the balance against the Fokker.

Fokker Stopper 1

The DH2, designed by Geoffrey de Havilland, was a pusher biplane. It looked painfully obsolete but, despite having a rear-mounted engine, it was a proper single-seat scout. With a speed of 85 mph (140 kph) at 7,000 feet 2,150 m), and a ceiling of 14,000 feet (4,300 m), the DH2 could outperform the Fokker – just. The pilot had a clear view in front of him and a fixed, forward-mounted machine gun.

Fokker Stopper 2
The French Nieuport Scout looked to the future with a front-mounted engine. It had a top speed of 107 mph (170 kph) and a ceiling of 17,400 feet (5,350 m). It was armed with a Lewis gun on top of the wing, firing safely over the propeller. It became the favourite plane of two top British aces, Albert Ball and James McCudden.

Fokker Stopper 3
Finally, in May 1916, the RFC began to receive the first British plane with a forward-mounted machine gun and an interrupter gear to fire through the propeller: the Sopwith 1^1/2 Strutter.

During the summer of 1916 the RFC regained command of the air, but it was a narrow lead that was soon to be challenged by a new generation of German aircraft.

RFC Aircraft

Type and country of origin	Crew and purpose	Speed	Weapons	Comments
Martinsyde S.I Britain	1 Fighter	87 mph (139 km) at sea level	One Lewis gun	A poor plane, withdrawn from service by mid-1915
Morane-Saulnier France	1 or 2 Fighter	71 mph (114 kph) at sea level	One fixed Lewis gun firing through the propeller	One of the first planes used for aerial combat
Nieuport 11 France 1	1 Fighter	97 mph (155 kph) at sea level	One fixed, forward firing Lewis gun, mounted above the upper wing	Nicknamed the Bébé (Baby), this was a highly manoeuvrable plane with a fast rate of climb
Sopwith 1½ Strutter Britain	2 Fighter, bomber and reconnaissance	106 mph (170 kph) at sea level	One fixed, forward-firing Vickers machine gun, one free-firing Lewis gun and up to 130 lb (59 kg) of bombs	A very successful fighter until it was outclassed by the German Albatros

German Aircraft

Type and country of origin	Crew and purpose	Speed	Weapons	Comments
Aviatik B and C Germany	2 Reconnaissance	89 mph (142 kph) at sea level	At first unarmed, the C.I was equipped with one forward-firing Parabellum machine gun	A successful plane in widespread use 1914–17
Etrich Taube Austria-Hungary and Germany	2 Reconnaissance and training	71 mph (142 kph) at sea level	None	A striking aircraft with a bird-like structure. Over 500 were built and the Taube stayed in service until 1916
Fokker EI Germany	1 Fighter	87 mph (139 kph) at sea level	One fixed, forward-firing machine gun	The plane that shocked the Allies in the summer of 1915. Pilots did not expect to be shot at by a plane approaching from behind

On the Wings of the Morning

A sudden roar, a mighty rushing sound,
a jolt or two, a smoothly sliding rise,
a tumbled blur of disappearing ground,
and all sense of motion slowly dies.
Quiet and calm the earth slips past below,
as underneath a bridge still waters flow.

My turning wing inclines towards the ground;
The ground itself glides up with graceful swing
and at the plane's far tip twirls slowly round,
then drops from sight again beneath the wing
to slip away serenely as before,
a cubist patterned carpet on the floor.

Hills gently sink and valleys gently fill.
The flattened fields grow ludicrously small;
slowly they pass underneath and slower still
until they hardly seem to move at all.
Then suddenly they disappear from sight,
hidden by fleeting wisps of faded white.

The wing-tips, faint and dripping, dimly show,
blurred by wreaths of mist that intervene.
Weird half-seen shadows flicker to and fro
across the pallid fog-bank's blinding screen.
At last the choking mists release their hold,
and all the world is silver, blue and gold.

Jeffrey Day

Note: Jeffrey flew for the Royal Navy Air Service. On 27 February 1918
he took on six enemy planes single-handed and was shot down and
killed

AIRSHIP KILLER

BATTLE BRIEFING

Aircraft were not the only way to take to the skies. Before the war, lighter-than-air technology seemed far more promising – and the Germans were the world leaders. By 1914, airships were gigantic yet graceful machines able to carry tons of cargo – or bombs – at a time when aircraft struggled to take off with one or two people. They had a range of over 1,000 miles (1,600 km), a speed of around 50–60 mph (80–96 kph) and an operational ceiling of about 13,000 feet (14,000 m). Crew quarters and engines were suspended from the framework while the huge bags of hydrogen gas, called balloonets, were carried inside. Hydrogen, a lighter-than-air gas, gave the airships their lift, but it was highly flammable.

The Death of New York

When the war began the British expected an immediate attack by enemy airships. For years there had been scare stories about the destruction that would rain from the skies. The top science-fiction writer H. G. Wells wrote a best-selling serial called The War in the Air. In this cracking adventure, a fleet of airships cross the Atlantic to destroy New York and smash the city, leaving it in ruins with many people dead.

Fuelled by fears like these, there was a spate of airship sightings and wild rumours of German spies. Something had to be done to reassure the public, but by September 1914 the RFC was busy in Europe. After some squabbling between the army and the navy, the air defence of Britain was handed over to the Royal Naval Air Service (RNAS).

Winston Churchill, then First Lord of the Admiralty (head of the navy), laid down the key features of a defence scheme:

- Anti-aircraft guns and searchlights were to protect key targets such as oil depots and docks.
- Interceptor squadrons of aircraft were to be based on the French and Belgian coasts to catch enemy airships before they reached Britain.
- London would be defended by a squadron of aeroplanes based at Hendon.
- Ordinary people must be given guidance about what to expect and police and fire brigades prepared. Plans must be made to turn off city lights.

Punch cartoon showing John Bull (Britain) giving German Zepplin a withering look
Zepplin (as 'The Fat Boy'): I wants to make your flesh creep.
John Bull: Right-o!

Slow in Coming

If the British were worried, the Germans were keen not to disappoint them. But they had problems. As often happens, speculation was far ahead of the facts. By August 1914 the German Army only had seven airships and three of these were soon shot down by ground fire over the battlefields of Belgium and France. The German Navy was even worse off. Out of three airships, two had accidentally gone up in flames, while the third had to be kept ready to support the High Seas fleet in any clash with the Royal Navy. It took months to build nine new Zeppelins ... but then the time to strike arrived.

WILD HAWK

First Strike

The first airship raid on England came on 19 January 1915. Three German Navy Zeppelins, L3, L4 and L6, set out for East Anglia on a night attack. L6 had to turn back with engine trouble, but the others flew on. They reached the Norfolk coast and dropped their bombs on Yarmouth before pushing inland to hit King's Lynn. Neither town had any important military targets and both were poorly defended against attack from the air. Four civilians were killed and a handful of homes destroyed.

The nation was shocked, but puzzled too. What on earth were these monsters after? The only sensible answer seemed too horrible. Surely, the papers argued, they must have been stalking the King and Queen. The royal estate at Sandringham was not far away and the royal family had only returned to London the day before. Had the Kaiser, the German emperor, stooped to this – sending airships by night to assassinate his cousins at their country home, where he had been a welcome guest before the war? True or not, it seemed like another German outrage!

The Times was to declare that this attack had brought to an end 'the age-long immunity of the heart of the British Empire from the sight of a foe and the sound of an enemy missile'. It also brought angry public demands for action. There had been lighting controls in London since

A Zeppelin (L32) in flight

the war began but the towns of East Anglia were brightly lit on that dark, winter night. Belatedly, the blackout was now extended across the South and the Midlands.

Worse, there were too few anti-aircraft guns to defend every potential target. In an unseemly hurry, a mobile force of lorries carrying machine guns, pom-poms and searchlights was formed. If the Zeppelins were spotted in time, perhaps by ships in the Channel or observers along the coast, these airship hunters would rush to block their path.

Target London

Yet, in spite of these precautions, the raids continued. The 'Zepps' seemed to move across the skies of England at will, and on 31 May 1915 London was attacked for the first time. LZ38 crossed the Channel and reached Stoke Newington, north-east London, before it was spotted at 23:20. As the airship soared over east London the crew dropped grenades and incendiary (fire) bombs on the houses below.

Once again, innocent civilians were the victims. Mrs C. Smith, living in Cowper Street, recalled:

> I had just got into bed when I heard a terrible rushing of wind and shouts of 'Fire' and 'The Germans are here'. I jumped out of bed and carried my four children into the basement and then went out to the street door and saw the house next door was on fire and people were

> *helping to get the children out. The father was burnt*
> *and the daughter, who my daughter used to play with,*
> *had met her death ...We later found the poor little dear*
> *had crawled under the bed to get away from the flames.*

LZ38 had dropped 3,000 lb (1,360 kg) of bombs, killed seven people and injured 35. More significantly, it had terrified the population of London. The Zeppelins looked deadly and sinister – like giant alien spacecraft might appear today. While their tiny payload could inflict only limited damage, they seemed far more dangerous to the people of a frightened city.

The little girl who died was called Elsie Leggett. Shortly afterwards, her sister Mary also died of her injuries. Grimly fascinated, thousands of Londoners paid a penny to walk through the remains of their home. Many must have wondered if they would be next – and they wanted revenge.

A Problem Pilot

On 7 May 1915 Lieutenant Reginald Warneford was posted to 1 Wing Royal Navy Air Service (see pages 67–8) The wing was stationed at St Pol airfield, near Dunkirk in France – the front line of England's air defence. The plan was simple: catch the Zepps leaving or returning to their bases in German-occupied Belgium. It was easier ordered than done.

The commander at St Pol was Arthur Longmore and he

was not the happiest of men. His new pilot was a rebel. He glanced down Warneford's record again and sighed.

Born in 1891 in India, the son of a civil engineer. Joined the merchant navy as a boy of 13. An officer in the Indian Steam Navigation Company when the war began. Volunteered for the Royal Navy Air Service in 1915. Stubborn . . . easily bored . . . irked by discipline . . . undoubtedly brave . . . As wild as a hawk.

Reginald Warneford

In a firm interview Longmore warned Reginald that he came to France with an 'unsavoury' reputation. 'I'll be keeping an eye on you, Warneford,' he said sternly. But, he continued in a more kindly tone, 'Think on it. This time you have a chance to start again. I will judge you solely on your behaviour in I Wing.' It seemed the advice fell on deaf ears. Only hours later Reginald was back in his office for a severe ticking-off. The Lieutenant had recklessly driven one of the airfield's few motor tenders into a ditch. Longmore later wrote:

He was one of the most astounding characters I ever met. Here was a case of a man who knew absolutely no fear, and my problem was to keep him alive as long as possible and use him to do the maximum damage against the Germans.

But sadly, 'as long as possible' didn't turn out to be that long …

Fighting Mad

The next day Reginald more than made up for his mistakes, dragging his unfortunate observer, John D'Albiac, with him! They were patrolling between Zeebrugge and Ostend when Reginald spotted a German reconnaissance plane and set off in pursuit. The enemy machine tried to lose him, skimming away at little more than rooftop height. Reginald was overjoyed – a challenge! Flying and firing his rifle at the same time, he chased the German plane back to base in Ostend, forcing the terrified crew to land.

When they got back to the RFC base John was fuming. The fuel tank was almost empty – in a few minutes they would have had to make an emergency landing. He complained to the CO that Reginald had ignored his signals that they were running out of petrol and put them both in peril with his wild heroics. He never wanted to be teemed up with 'this madman' again.

In the coming weeks Reginald was equally unstoppable,

attacking any German aircraft that came along and bombing troop and gun positions. Longmore was impressed and decided to give Reginald 'free rein' to seek his own targets. Better still, the commander got hold of the best weapon he could for his 'wild hawk' – a Morane Saulnier monoplane. This single-seater French aircraft had deflector plates fitted to the propellers (see pages 44–5) and Reginald was one of the first British pilots to be given a crack at the new plane.

The Death of L37

On the evening of 6 June 1915 Longmore received a message from the Admiralty: three airships that had just attacked England were returning to base. At once he ordered two pilots from 1 Wing to bomb the airship sheds at Evere in Belgium, while Reginald was sent up to see what he could find. He took off at 01:00 on 7 June, his Morane Saulnier loaded with six 20-lb (9-kg) bombs strapped under the fuselage.

That short summer night Reginald's luck was in. He had only been in the air a few minutes when he caught sight of his prey. In the far distance was a German Army airship. Later he learned that this was LZ37, commanded by Oberleutnant von der Haegen, with a crew of 28 on board. LZ37 had set out on a night raid with two other airships but they had all turned back due to poor weather. More surprisingly, LZ37 was not one of the airships the Admiralty had mentioned – Reginald ran into the lone airship by pure chance.

At first it seemed that the Zepp would get away. It took Reginald 45 minutes of hard flying to catch up with his giant opponent. It was 01:50, somewhere near Bruges, when they began their David and Goliath battle in the air. Reginald closed in but was met by a blast of machine-gun fire and banked away, trying to gain height. As he wheeled aside von der Haegen swung the nose of the airship after him. It turned into a game of cat and mouse as the German gunners tried to swat the buzzing aircraft, while Reginald tried to climb out of range.

For 20 minutes the opponents manoeuvred in the dark, then abruptly LZ37 stopped firing and turned

Reginald Warneford attacking a Zeppelin

towards base. Perhaps von der Haegen felt the enemy pilot had tried his best and was not a real threat. He was wrong!

Reginald had slowly climbed to 11,000 feet (3,400 m) and, switching off his engine, dived to the attack. At 7,000 feet (2,150 m) and barely 150 feet (45 m) above the enemy, he began his bombing run. Coming in from the stern, he skimmed the length of the airship with no effect. Were his bombs duds? But as the sixth and last was released, an explosion tore across the forward section of LZ37.

The next moments were like a vision of hell. The stricken Zeppelin began to disintegrate in mid-air. Burning hydrogen gas belched into the night, like an erupting volcano. In 6 seconds the broken hulk of the airship plunged to the ground, raining a fearsome litter of smashed framework and burning fabric.

The Human Cost

Slung underneath their ship in two control cars, the crew realized the ship was on fire. Some leapt into the air to escape the flames, while others clung on frantically. Tragically LZ37 did not fall into open fields. The wreckage crashed on to a convent in the suburbs of Ghent. Two nuns, a man and a child were killed, while others were seriously injured.

Yet amazingly one crewman survived. Arthur Muhler, the ship's coxswain (he steered the airship), fell through the roof of the convent and landed in a bed. He escaped with burns, bruising and shock – and a harrowing tale:

The men in the forward control car were the first to feel the great shudder of the explosion. Above us the vast envelope quivered and began to wrinkle and collapse. The wheel went dead in my hands and the gondola trembled. All around were shouts and confused orders. I saw dark shapes of men silhouetted against a ruddy glow, their flailing hands trying to protect their faces. Some of them climbed over the sides of the car and flung themselves into space. I could not make myself let go of the wheel. I clung to it like a drowning man until it broke in my hands. I was flung to the floor. The scorching heat increased and increased and our clothes burst into flames. The gondola began to tilt and rock until, with a terrible sound of breaking wood and metal, it tore away from the main structure and plunged towards the ground. I knew no more until I woke up in hospital.

As the airship blew up, Reginald's joy was short-lived. His plane was caught in the blast, flipped on its back and hurtled upwards for 200 feet (60 m). It wasn't until the Morane dropped into a nosedive that the controls finally responded. But the danger was far from over. Reginald couldn't restart the engine and he was over enemy-occupied territory. There was nothing for it but to try an emergency landing.

He landed in a field next to a farmhouse and put his hand on his revolver. Surely, with the sky lit up brighter than Blackpool illuminations, the area would be crawling with troops? Frantically Reginald inspected his engine and found that a fuel feed line from the rear tank to the pump had split. It took 15 heart-stopping minutes to complete running repairs, but there was another more basic problem. It usually took two men to start a plane. In his report he recalled his frantic take-off:

Without another chap I could not keep the engine running long enough for me to get back into the cockpit – I was pretty desperate by then. I pulled and pushed and bounced her along until I got her nose pointing down a steep hill. Then I swung the prop. I kept on hauling and pushing – she started to move slowly at first and then as she gathered speed I knew she wouldn't stop. I made a leap for the cockpit just as the **Boche** *charged out of the wood firing in my direction.*

Yet Reginald was still not safe. The weather had worsened and now thick mist and fog were hiding the ground. Unable to get his bearings, he headed south-west. With no idea where he was and with fuel running out, the tired pilot had to play a dangerous game. From time to time he dropped into the fog, almost hugging the ground, to look for landmarks. Finally, his petrol exhausted, he landed on the sands at Cap Gris-Nez to wait for daylight. When the sun came up he was refuelled by a French unit and returned to St Pol at 10:30.

Warneford, VC

Within days Reginald had become a national hero. For the first time an airship had been shot down by an aeroplane. He received a telegraph from the Admiralty, carrying the personal congratulations of King George V, and the stunning news that he was to be awarded the Victoria Cross. On 9 June the French government announced that he was to be made a Chevalier de Legion d'Honneur.

Commander Longmore was delighted. His faith in Reginald had been justified, and of course this was a feather in the cap of the whole RNAS. Proudly he gave the lieutenant leave to collect the French decoration in Paris. And while he was there, the commander asked, would he be good enough to fly back a new plane for the wing – a Henri Farman.

On Thursday 17 June Reginald received the Legion d'Honneur from none other than General Joffre – known as 'Papa' Joffre, the saviour of France at the Battle of the Marne in 1914. This was followed by a slap-up lunch, after which he went out to Buc airfield to pick up the Farman. Always eager to try new machines, he decided to see what it could do. With an American on board, a journalist eager for a flight with the hero of the moment, Reginald put on a show. He banked and turned through a series of violent manoeuvres, then dived at full power from 1,000 feet (300 m) to zoom over the heads of the admiring crowd.

Abruptly, the perfect day ended. As the Farman climbed out of the dive the wings buckled, the propeller hit the tail boom and the plane disintegrated. Both the pilot and the passenger were catapulted out of the cockpit and plummeted 200 feet (60 m) to earth. Shocked spectators rushed to the scene of the crash and found the journalist dead but Reginald still breathing. Horribly, the Legion d'Honneur had been driven into his chest by the impact. Lieutenant Warneford was rushed to hospital but died of his injuries on the way. The wild hawk was down.

FIGHTING FACTS

RNAS and RFC – Rivals in the Sky
The RFC was set up in 1912 with a military wing to serve with the army and a naval wing to meet the needs of the Royal Navy. From the start, however, the navy wanted control of its own aircraft and soon changed the name of the naval wing to the RNAS. This left the army in sole control of the RFC. Unwisely the RNAS and RFC became rivals, competing for resources and manpower. In 1918 both were merged into the new Royal Air

Force. The RAF became Britain's third armed service, independent of both the army and the navy.

Tolerable Terminology

Like the British Army and the Royal Navy, the German armed services were rivals. The German Navy bought airships from the company owned by Cavalry Officer Graf (Count) von Zeppelin. They were designated L at first or LZ for the larger machines made later in the war. Zeppelins had an aluminium skeleton covered with fabric.

The German Army bought similar airships from a competing firm, Luftschiffbau (*luft*, air; *schiff*, ship) Schutte-Lanz. They were designated SL. The major difference was SLs had a plywood framework instead of a metal one.

These subtleties were lost on the British, however. All enemy airships soon became known as Zeppelins or Zepps, regardless of who made them. (Just like vacuum cleaners today are sometimes called Hoovers, even though Hoover is just one make.)

In this story the term 'Zeppelin' is used loosely to describe any German airship. However, some people can get very worked up about this and, strictly speaking, it's wrong. One writer has attacked 'the welter of ignorance and confusion into which the terminology of lighter-than-air flight has fallen'. But you won't tread on any toes if you know your Zepp from your Schutte-Lanz.

LZ38

Remember the two other pilots who set off on a mission on 7 June? John Wilson and John Mills were ordered to bomb the airship sheds at Evere. They not only found their target in a night raid, they dodged the enemy guns and hit hard. One shed burned down with LZ38 inside – the same airship that had bombed London only the week before!

1916 – Terror from the Skies 2

In 1916, reinforced by a new generation of Zeppelins, the Germans attacked again. The latest ships carried more hydrogen and far more bombs. Peter Strasser, the Leader of Airships, was out to show that his crews could drop enough explosives to damage the British war effort.

The British responded by improving their defences, posting squadrons at key locations down the eastern half of the country. Crucially, the planes were equipped with new ammunition. Throughout 1915 pilots had blazed away with their Lewis guns without any obvious effect. The bullets had simply passed straight through the hydrogen bags, causing nothing but irritating leaks that were quickly patched by the sailmakers aboard the Zepps. It sounds zany, but the Germans had crewmen stitching up holes even while the airships were under attack.

Now the British machine guns fired a deadly mix of Brock or Pomeroy explosive bullets and Buckingham incendiary bullets. (Named after their inventors. Brock also manufactured fireworks.) They made a lethal combination when fired together. The explosive bullets blew holes in the Zeppelin gas bags, allowing the hydrogen to mix with the oxygen in the air. The incendiary bullets then ignited the mixed gases. Result – BOOM! After a long and lucky run against British aircraft, the Germans were in for a shock.

Zeppelin Down

Shortly after 23:00 on 2 September 1916 Lieutenant 'Billy' Leefe Robinson took off from Sutton Farm airfield, near London. A Zeppelin alert had sent the pilots scurrying into the air and he hoped for some action! Climbing his BE2c night-fighter through thick cloud, he levelled off at 3,000 feet (920 m) to patrol between Hornchurch and Joyce Green near Dartford Marshes. After a couple of mind-numbing hours his bleary eyes caught a sharp gleam of light to the east – a Zepp trapped in the beam of a searchlight.

Opening the throttle, Billy set off in hot pursuit. But his excitement soon faded. Long before he was in range, the airship slipped away into the clouds. Ho-hum. Boredom again. What are the chances of spotting two Zepps in one night? Billy wondered. 'None!' he moaned, giving a dismal answer to his own question.

Flying on, in the vain hope that the searchlights might catch another intruder, his wish was suddenly granted.

A Zepplin being shot down was a cause of celebration for the Allies

Luck: There it was – SL11. Visible in the flashes of . . .

Bad luck: . . . an intense bombardment of exploding anti-aircraft shells.

Despite the high risk of being shot down by his own side, Billy attacked. As SL11 twisted and turned to escape the ground-fire, he raked the full length of the underbelly with a whole drum of incendiaries.

But nothing happened!

Reloading his Lewis gun, he turned and dived along one side of the airship, again emptying a full drum into the giant.

Still nothing happened!

Could it be that Zepps really were invulnerable?

Attacking a third time, Billy changed his tactics. He put his plane behind and below SL11's massive **elevators** and pumped his last drum into a small area. This time, as the bullets ripped into the airship's frame, a dull pink glow bloomed deep inside the hull. Within seconds flames 100 feet (30 m) long shot out of the doomed raider.

As hot debris fell about him, Billy wrenched his aircraft out of the way. SL11 became a ball of fire visible from 35 miles (56 km) away, before it exploded and hit the ground at Cuffley, a small hamlet in Hertfordshire. This was the show Londoners had waited months to see. They poured out into the streets, singing and clapping as the airship died overhead. One witness was ten-year-old Henry Turtle, living in Islington. He remembered:

This newspaper illustration mirrors the British public's
horror of Zeppelin attacks on civilian targets

We opened the front door and there it was: a fantastic sight like a big silver cigar ... then all of a sudden flames started to come from the Zeppelin and it broke in half and was one mass of flames. It was an incredible sight: people were cheering, dancing and someone started playing the bagpipes. All the children, and I was one of them marched up and down cheering like merry hell. We were told afterwards, at school that the Zepp was shot down by Lt. Robinson RFC.

Flu Victim

Billy was awarded the Victoria Cross, the first for an action over or on British soil. Yet even heroes are helpless in the face of tiny foes – bugs. In 1918 the worst flu epidemic in history hit Britain. Over 150,000 people died and one of them was Billy Robinson.

Air Raid

Night shatters in mid-heaven – the bark of guns,
The roar of planes, the crash of bombs, and all
The unshackled skyey pandemonium stuns
The senses to indifference, when a fall
Of masonry nearby startles awake,
Tingling, wide-eyed, prick eared, with bristling hair,
Each sense within the body, crouched aware
Like some sore-hunted creature in the brake.

Yet side by side we lie in the little room,
Just touching hands, with eyes and ears that strain
Keenly, yet dream-bewildered, through tense gloom,
Listening, in helpless stupor of insane
Drugged nightmare panic fantastically wild,
To the quiet breathing of our little child.

Wilfrid Gibson

GOTHA
SUMMER

BATTLE BRIEFING

The Zeppelin raids of 1916 were beaten off with heavy German losses. Together with SL11, a string of other Zeppelins were soon destroyed, including:

- *L33 – brought down by ground fire over Bromley, Kent, on 23 September. When it crash-landed in Essex, the crew jumped to safety and set fire to their ship to prevent its capture.*
- *L32 – snared in searchlights over east London and shot down by Lieutenant Frederick Sowrey during the same raid.*
- *L31 – shot down over London by Second Lieutenant W. J. Tempest on 2 October. It crashed in flames at Potters Bar, Hertfordshire, and all the crew died. The captain was found embedded in the ground. He was still alive, though soon died of his injuries.*

After this gory autumn the myth of the invulnerable airship had been shattered. Even the bravest German crews were daunted and airship raids were scaled back.

As the Zeppelin threat faded, the British dropped their guard. Key pilots from home-defence squadrons were sent to the Western Front, while many of the anti-aircraft guns were fitted to merchant ships for the bitter war against the U-boats (submarines) in the Atlantic.

To release more men for the army – gunners, observers, searchlight operators, etc. could all be retrained as infantrymen – only guns stationed on the coast were allowed to open fire on intruders. Inland anti-aircraft batteries were ordered not to engage the enemy. One explanation for this amazing order was overconfidence. Home Forces Command did not expect a large attack, believing that the German Air Force was simply not up to it. Ironically, just as the British relaxed, the threat from the air was about to take a turn for the worse. By May 1917 the first squadrons of massive Gotha GIV bombers were finally ready and waiting.

THE SLAUGHTER OF THE INNOCENTS

High Stakes

By November 1916 the epic Battle of the Somme had ground to a halt. The British and French had taken a miserable strip of land 30 miles (50 km) long and 7 miles (11 km) deep – at a cost of 600,000 killed, wounded or captured. The terrible waste of young lives made the Somme a bitter symbol of the horror of war. But amidst the carnage there was some gain – German losses were almost as bad. The Kaiser's army was exhausted and needed time to recover and rebuild defences.

To gain time, the German High Command ordered two counter-strokes. The deadliest was at sea. U-boats were ordered to attack and sink enemy ships without mercy. It almost worked. During the spring of 1917 British shipping losses trebled and the war hung in the balance.

To pile on the pressure, and perhaps force the enemy to seek peace, the air force was ordered to attack London, the heart of the Allied war effort. General Ludendorff, a key player in the German High Command, wrote:

> *The plan was to take from the Allies their faith in victory. The main object was the moral intimidation of the British nation and the crippling of the will to fight.*

Crucial targets included government buildings around Downing Street, the Admiralty (HQ of the navy) and the Bank of England. And if nothing else, more air raids would force the British to divert men and resources from the Western Front to home defence.

A New Weapon

To deliver the blow, a crack unit was equipped with the latest long-range planes. Kampfgeschwader I (Battle Squadron I, shortened to Kagohl I and, just to complicate matters, renamed Kagohl 3) had aerodromes at St Denis Westrem and Melle-Gontrode, near Ghent, in Belgium. Led by an inspiring commander, Hauptmann Ernest Brandenburg, the pilots had been eager to have a crack at London since 1914. And now they were being given the tool to do it.

The GIV biplane bomber was nicknamed the Gotha after the company who made it, Gothaer Waggonfabrik AG. It was an awesome size. The fuselage was over 40 feet long (12 m) and the wingspan almost 78 feet (24 m). Powered by two 260-hp (horsepower) Mercedes engines, it had a maximum speed of 87 mph (140 kph) at 12,000 feet (3,700 m). The crew of three sat in a roomy cockpit, with a walkway between the seats. At the front was the commander. And just to make sure he had no time for dozing, he was also observer/navigator/bomb aimer and front gunner. Next came the pilot and behind him sat the rear gunner.

The GIV was armed with three 7.92-mm Parabellum machine guns, one at the front and two at the back. This clever design gave the rear gunner a choice of weapons and proved a nasty shock to British pilots attacking from behind. One gun was mounted to fire above the fuselage, but the second swivelled to shoot through a

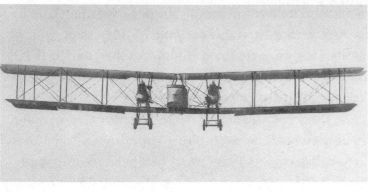

The Gotha G5

tunnel, spraying the area under the tail. To make sure they didn't freeze up at high altitudes, the guns were electrically heated, the power coming from a dynamo driven by the right-hand engine. The ammo drums held 200 rounds.

The bomb load depended upon the height of a raid. During the day the Gotha attacked from as high as 18,000 feet (5,540 m) and could only carry 700 lb (320 kg) of bombs. At night, when it flew lower, at 10,000 feet (3,080 m), the load was increased to 1,000 lb (455 kg). In early raids, the heaviest German bombs weighed 110 lb (50 kg) but, luckily for London, poor fuses meant that a third of those dropped were duds, while another 10 per cent exploded in the air.

First Raids
By mid-May 1917 the pilots of Kagohl 3 were fully

trained and itching for action, but poor weather held up the first attack. It was not until 25 May that days of thunderstorms passed and the sun shone. At 15:30 the bombers lumbered into the air and set course for England.

The main target was London, but as the Gothas came in over Essex, Brandenburg saw that the capital was hidden by dense cloud. Disappointed, but determined to hit the enemy hard, he fired signal flares to turn his force south into Kent. At 16:30 half the force attacked Shorncliffe Camp, a huge undefended army base full of Canadian troops. Twenty-seven bombs were dropped, one falling on a company of soldiers preparing for an evening route march. There was carnage among the neat, unsuspecting ranks – 17 were killed and 93 wounded.

A few minutes later the raiders hit Folkestone. It was Friday evening, pay night, just before the Whitsun holiday, and the streets were packed with shoppers. One bomb fell in the queue outside Stokes Grocer's, killing or seriously injuring 60 people, many of them children.

The Gothas had first been sighted at 16:45, yet for almost 2 hours they roamed through English airspace at will. Defences had been poorly coordinated and most anti-aircraft guns had obeyed the order not to open fire. Few gunners had realized this was a serious attack, not just a pin-prick raid by a couple of aircraft. Navy fighters did manage to shoot down two Gothas, but the rest of Kagohl 3 escaped almost without a scratch. Exactly as

the Germans planned, the British public were shocked –
and a little scared.

Target London

A second Gotha raid set out for London on 5 June, but
this time British defences were much sharper. Faced
with heavy anti-aircraft fire, the bombers turned instead
towards their back-up target, the dockyard town of
Sheerness. In a 5-minute attack, 13 people died and
another 34 were injured. Gotha 660 was shot down into
the sea.

A week later, on Wednesday 13 June, Kagohl 3 tried
again. This time the forecasters promised perfect flying
weather until late afternoon, when thunderstorms
would break. To make best use of the day, the squadron
took off from Belgium at 09:00. They would reach
London at midday, when the British capital was at its
busiest, and be back home before the weather broke.

By 10:30 20 raiders were nearing the North Foreland,
near Shoeburyness, and since this was the third assault
they expected a hard time from the enemy defences.
However, to create as much confusion as possible,
Brandenburg had prepared a double-decoy. He raised his
flare-gun into the slipstream and fired – a prearranged
signal for a lone machine to peel off and bomb Margate.
At 10:45 the pilot began his attack run and dropped four
bombs, causing little damage. But this didn't matter. He
had raised a hornet's nest and set off for home, chased

by nine vital fighters from Manston aerodrome. None was back in time to intercept the main force.

At 10:50, as the Gothas approached the Essex coast near the mouth of the River Crouch, two more planes left the formation and attacked Shoeburyness. This time the ruse failed. The bombers turned for home without any British fighters in pursuit.

By about 11:40 the Germans were wheeling over central London. The weather was perfect for the raiders – patchy cloud at about 5,000 feet (1,540 m), making it hard for anti-aircraft gunners to get a clear shot. Yet, viewed from 14,000 feet (4,300 m), the sparkling glass

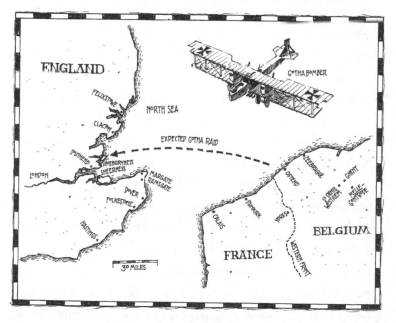

The route the Gotha bombers took

roof of Liverpool Street station shone like a navigation beacon in the hazy sunshine.

On the streets below, Londoners heard the drone of engines but were still unaware of the danger. One RFC pilot, Lieutenant Charles Chabot was among the crowds.

I was up in town on a day's leave ... wandering as an ordinary civilian down Cheapside ... when the raid started. Raids hadn't become a very serious thing and everybody crowded into the street to watch. They didn't take cover or dodge. A bomb went off right over the Guildhall and it seemed to me, having had quite a bit of experience of dropping bombs myself, that it was very disappointing for the chap who had thrown it at the Guildhall. It had gone off two or three hundred feet overhead. I couldn't help saying, 'Oh bad luck!' ... I saw I had said quite the wrong thing and had to make off.

But the Guildhall bomb was not typical and many found their mark. Two 110-lb (50-kg) bombs smashed down on the Royal Albert Dock, killing eight workers; three bombs landed on Liverpool Street station, wrecking two trains and killing 16 railwaymen and passengers; in Fenchurch Street a four-storey building was destroyed and 20 people died; in Aldgate High Street a bomb burst on the pavement, killing 13 and injuring another 22.

The grimmest tragedy, however, happened in Poplar. Five 110-lb (50-kg) bombs were dropped and one scored a direct hit on Upper North Street School. Miss

I. A. Major remembered the raiders passing overhead:

Our teachers had been warned of an approaching air raid and were endeavouring to keep us all calm by getting us to sing together. Soon, however, the noise of the anti-aircraft guns and the detonation of the enemy bombs sounded above even our shrill voices.

The bomb crashed through three floors and exploded in the infants' class on the ground floor, where 64 children had gathered. Esther Levy was in a nearby classroom. She recalled:

There was a tremendous bang and of course everybody was panic-stricken. A big fat girl called Kitty Chalmers fell on top of me ... but I picked myself up. The teachers were marvellous. They were saying 'Don't panic' and 'File down quietly' ... I distinctly remember one of the teachers carrying a girl – I think her name was Pittard – whose leg was severed. What really frightened me was seeing all those little children being carried out. They were all black and their hair ginger from TNT [explosive].

Rescue workers were shocked by the carnage they found in the school. Eighteen children were killed outright and another 30 had terrible injuries. Mrs Myers, then an older pupil, desperately looked for her younger sister in the wreckage of the school:

I forced my way along the corridor filled with men and

women frantically searching for their children. All were
screaming and shouting. I could not find her anywhere
and it was two hours later when my father found her
dead in the mortuary.

Telegraphic Address:
"Schools, Estrand, London."
Telephone No.
10,000 Gerrard.

London County Council.

AT THE HEAD
OF YOUR REPLY
PLEASE WRITE

Education Offices,
Victoria Embankment, W.C. 2.

20th June, 1917.

Dear Mr. Brewis,

As Chairman of the Education Committee for London I
feel that I must write you a few lines of heartfelt sympathy.
The injury to your little girl Catherine through the sudden and
terrifying disaster of last Wednesday, 13th June, must have been
a very severe blow to you. It may, however, be some comfort to
you to know that so many people are thinking of you in your
trouble. In the days to come your little girl will be remembered
as one who suffered for her country just as much as if she had
been a soldier wounded while fighting at the front. My sincere
sympathy is with you.

The Minister for Education, Mr. Herbert Fisher, asks
me to convey to you his warmest sympathy.

Yours very sincerely,

[signature]

Chairman of the Education Committee.

Mr. J. G. Brewis,
54, Gough Street,
E.14.

A letter of sympathy to the parents of a girl wounded in the bombing of Upper North
Street School, east London, in June 1917

86

A Disgrace to the Empire

By midday the Gothas had finished their attack and were approaching Southend, on their way back to Belgium. They had run the gauntlet of anti-aircraft guns but none had been hit. More humiliating for the British, over 90 RFC fighters took off to catch Kagohl 3, yet only 12 came close enough to open fire. And even these were soon outdistanced by the German planes, travelling higher and faster since they had dropped their bombs.

One of those taking part in the hunt was Captain James McCudden, by now a proud pilot. He wrote a vivid account of the maddening action:

I took off in an easterly direction. At 5,000 feet I climbed into woolly clouds and not until I reached 10,000 feet did I see the ground again through small gaps between the clouds. It was an ideal day for a bombing formation to get to their objective unobserved.

I caught up with them at the expense of some height and by the time I got under the rear machine I was 1,000 feet below. I now found that there were over 20 machines, all with two 'pusher' engines. To my dismay I could not lessen the range to any appreciable extent. By the time I had got to 500 feet under the rear machine we were 20 miles off the Essex coast, and visions of a very long swim entered my mind, so I decided to fire all my ammunition and then depart.

I fired my first drum, of which the Hun did not take

the slightest notice. I now perceived another Sopwith
Pup just behind this rear Hun at quite close range, but
after a while he turned away as though he was
experiencing some trouble with his gun.

How insolent these damn Boches did look, absolutely
lording the sky above England! I replaced my first drum
with another and had another try, after which the Hun
swerved ever so slightly, and that welcome sound of
machine-guns smote my ears and I caught the smell of
the Hun's incendiary bullets as they passed me. I now
put on my third and last single Lewis drum [each drum
held 47 shots] and fired again. To my intense chagrin,
the last Hun did not take the slightest notice.

The Gothas' luck held all the way home. RNAS fighters from Dunkirk had been **scrambled** but failed to spot the returning bombers. At about 14:00 Kagohl 3 landed at its bases without mishap. Half an hour later the weather broke in a furious storm, with heavy rain and hailstones as large as pigeon's eggs. If the British defences had simply managed to slow down the Gothas, then they would have been caught in that maelstrom and several most likely wrecked.

Brandenburg was delighted with the results of the raid. His airmen had certainly wrenched the tail of the British lion, just as Ludendorff had ordered. And they had created a wave of terror – 162 people were killed and 432 injured, the most punishing raid of the whole war. In London there was outrage that 16 enemy bombers could roam at will over the capital of the greatest empire on earth without being challenged. 'What has gone wrong?' the newspapers demanded. 'And what is being done about it?'

FIGHTING FACTS

The Carrier Pigeon Squadron

Bombing London using aeroplanes had always been part of German plans to win the war. In 1914 Major General Siegert, a former balloon pilot, took charge of just such a force. It was codenamed the Carrier Pigeon Squadron to fool enemy spies. He faced two problems:

One: The 36 B-type bombers he was given were underpowered and could carry only small loads.

Two: The B-types had a short range and needed an airfield near Calais if they were to reach London. Siegert was robbed of this when the German advance was stopped in October 1914. Bases were set up in Belgium but they were too far away. The Carrier Pigeon Squadron had to make do with attacks on Allied aerodromes on the Western Front.

The plan to bomb London was filed away but not forgotten. The German Air Force issued specifications for a Grosskampfflugzeug (a large bomber aircraft) – the

G-type – and several companies, including Gothaer Waggonfabrik AG, set to work on designs.

The Blue Max

When Kagohl 3 landed back in Belgium on 13 June 1917, it was to a hero's welcome. Kaiser Wilhelm II was delighted with the results of the attack and ordered that Hauptmann Brandenburg be presented to him at Supreme Headquarters at Kreuznach in southern Germany.

The following day Brandenburg flew the 200 miles (320 km) to Kreuznach in a two-seater Albatros, piloted by Oberleutnant von Trotha. The meeting went well. The Kaiser listened closely to Brandenburg's tale of the raid and presented him with the Blue Max – the highly prized medal held by top German aces like Max Immelman and Manfred von Richthofen, known as the Red Baron.

Early on the morning of Tuesday 19 June, with von Trotha at the controls again, Brandenburg set out to return to Kagohl 3. Shortly after take-off the engine stalled and the Albatros spun to earth. The pilot died instantly and Brandenburg was severely injured – his legs crushed. Sheer bad luck had achieved more than the combined efforts of all the British defences. Kagohl 3 had lost a great leader – and never performed as well again as a fighting unit.

Losing the Propaganda War

At first the Germans were thrilled with the results of

the 13 June raid. An apology was sent for the deaths of the civilians, especially the children. The message nevertheless went on to blame the British government for these unnecessary losses, saying residents should have been moved away from military targets such as Sheerness and London.

In reality the German High Command knew that attacks on England would cause civilian casualties – and considered this no bad thing. It was believed this would add to the terror of the raids and shake British morale. The only German newspaper to condemn the attacks on London was closed down.

But the plan backfired. The British people were shocked and horrified by the deaths of the Poplar children. It was the worst outrage since the sinking of the passenger liner *Lusitania* by a U-boat in 1915. The tragedy seemed to prove that the war against such a barbaric enemy *had* to be won. Far from weakening the fighting spirit of the British, the Germans found they had rekindled it.

Duff Defence

The defence of London had been a shambles. The list of clangers was a long one:

* Too many British home-defence fighters were old-fashioned machines like the BE2c, the FE2b and the BE12. They were fine for tackling Zeppelins at night but not much else. Even the best of them, the BE12, could only just claw its way to 13,000 feet (4,000 m) –

not high enough to catch the Gothas. Only a handful of fighters – Sopwith 1^1/2 Strutters, Camels or Pups – had the speed and ceiling to bring the bombers down. If they could intercept in time ...

- Attack warnings took too long to reach fighter airfields. By the time the fighters had scrambled and climbed to 14,000 feet (4,300 m), the Gothas were already on their way home.
- Home-defence pilots were used to operating on their own at night. They had little experience of working together against armed formations of enemy planes. During the raid on 13 June, 94 fighters took off to intercept the Gothas, but only 12 came close enough to open fire. None of the pilots coordinated an attack with another aircraft.
- British machine guns jammed too often because of faulty ammunition. Flight Lieutenant Fox, flying a Sopwith Pup, attacked a Gotha at 14,000 feet over Southend. His tracer bullets were licking the enemy fuselage when his Lewis gun seized up. Furious, all he could do was drop out of the fight.
- Anti-aircraft fire had been piecemeal and inaccurate. No enemy planes were hit, but at least one British fighter had been badly damaged. Worse, two people were killed and 18 others injured by falling shell splinters. This had happened because their cases were not blown into small enough pieces when shells exploded.

- Air-raid warnings were given only to people working in likely targets, to avoid disrupting war work and causing panic. Some civilian casualties occurred among people who had poured out on to the streets to look at the Gothas flying overhead.

Getting It Right

The Germans had been wrong about the Gotha raids sapping Britain's will to fight. But they were correct about forcing the British to use up valuable resources to defend their capital city. Faced with a huge public outcry, the government responded with a number of urgent improvements to home defence.

- **Improvement:** The London Air Defence Area was set up to pull together control of air-raid warnings, fighters, guns and searchlights. Aeroplanes fitted with radios patrolled the skies to track bomber formations and report their speed and direction. An operations room plotted incoming raiders on a large squared map and direct telephone lines were installed to warn airfields and gun sites.
- **Improvement:** Three new squadrons of top-class fighters were formed − but at a cost! The men and machines were urgently needed in France, where losses were mounting calamitously. By August 1917 a further 150 new fighters had been delivered to other units.

- **Improvement:** The Green Line – a ring of anti-aircraft guns round the east of London – was set up to fire a mass of exploding shells at incoming bombers. It was hoped that this barrage would break up the tight formations of Gothas and make them easier prey for fighters.
- **Improvement:** Air-raid warnings were given over a large area using rockets and policemen blowing whistles. Sirens, unlike those used in World War II, were not loud enough to be heard over the roar of London traffic.

An Irish Airman Foresees His Death

I know that I shall meet my fate
Somewhere among the clouds above;
Those that I fight I do not hate,
Those that I guard I do not love;
My country is Kiltartan Cross,
My countrymen Kiltartan's poor,
No likely end could bring them loss
Or leave them happier than before.
Nor law, nor duty bade me fight,
Nor public men, nor cheering crowds,
A lonely impulse of delight
Drove to this tumult in the clouds;
I balanced all, brought all to mind,
The years to come seemed waste of breath,
A waste of breath the years behind
In balance with this life, this death.

W. B. Yeats

ACE OF ACES

BATTLE BRIEFING

The Somme

On 1 July 1916 the British Army began the great attack on the Somme. A massive bombardment had swept enemy lines for days, firing over 1,700,000 shells. The troops were told that this would destroy the German defences and that the advance would be a walkover. It wasn't. On the first day of the 'big push' 57,000 men were killed or injured – and the battle rolled grimly on until 18 November.

During the long Somme campaign the RFC did everything that was asked of it . . . and more. The 'Fokker scourge' was beaten and for most of the battle British planes controlled the skies. With the arrival of faster fighters, like the DH2 and the Sopwith Pup, the RFC developed new tactics. Orders stated that scouts should stay close to the reconnaissance machines they were protecting, but some plucky pilots realized that it was more efficient to go 'looking for the enemy rather than waiting for him to find you'.

In their battered trenches the infantry had a worm's-eye view of the fighting in the air. Captain Arthur Gibbs of the Welsh Guards wrote:

> Our aeroplanes are magnificent all day and every day. They fly low over our line, and the Boche line, and see exactly where we are and what is going on … Any Boche plane that puts its nose out of port is jolly soon chased back again.

Even the German High Command admitted in a frank report:

> The first weeks of the Somme battle were marked by the complete inferiority of our own air forces. The enemy's aeroplanes enjoyed complete freedom in carrying out distant reconnaissances. With the aid of aeroplane observation, the hostile artillery neutralized our guns and was able to range with extreme accuracy on the trenches occupied by our infantry.

The Albatros

When the German reply came, it was deadly. Reinforcements flooded into the Somme sector but, crucially, their scouts were organized into new hunting or fighting squadrons called Jastas. Pilots were no longer lone wolves but operated in killer teams of 14 machines.

Worse still for the British, in September 1916 a new German plane reached the battlefront – the Albatros DI. This was a brilliant aircraft, fitted with two synchronized machine guns firing through the propeller arc. The 160-hp Mercedes engines gave a top speed of 105 mph (168 kph) and a ceiling of 14,000 feet (4,300 m). Soon, the balance of power in the air flipped back to Germany and the RFC suffered heavily. During the Somme campaign 359 German planes were destroyed and 43 pilots killed at a cost of 800 British machines and 252 RFC pilots.

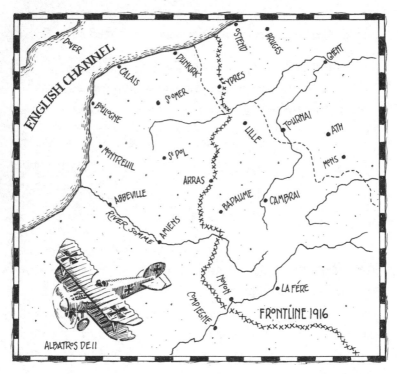

France, 1916

Arras

In April 1917 the British Fifth Army began a new offensive near Arras and once again the RFC was ordered to sweep the skies of German aircraft. But this time the plan went dreadfully wrong. Now 37 Jastas patrolled enemy lines. The pilots had been hand-picked for their skills in single-seater fighters and most flew the Albatros, including the latest – DIII.

As the British reconnaissance machines and their guarding scouts flew over German lines, the Jastas climbed into the sun and waited. The up-and-coming ace, Manfred von Richthofen wrote:

It is better if the customers come to the shop. Certainly they are brave, but it is a bravery with a touch of foolishness about it.

The air battle over Arras would be remembered as 'Bloody April' by the RFC. One hundred and fifty planes were shot down, 28 on Easter Sunday alone. The flying life of a fighter pilot fell to $17^1/2$ hours. And in the months that followed the slaughter continued. Into this butchery flew one man who soon became a match for the best German aces – Edward 'Mick' Mannock. However the first weeks of his career were anything but promising.

MICK MANNOCK – THE MAKING OF AN ACE

Too Cocky by Half

Have you ever been in the wrong place at the wrong time? Or been in trouble because you've got a big mouth? Then you may feel a little sympathy for Mick Mannock. On 6 April 1917 he suffered from both problems when he joined 40 Squadron at their base at Aire in France. Unfortunately, first impressions do count and the poor showing Mick made that day dogged him for weeks.

At best, 6 April was a bad day to join the squadron. They had just been in action and been badly mauled by the Germans, losing a popular pilot, Lieutenant Pell. The mood in the mess was dour and the last thing they needed was an insensitive jerk. Enter the new boy, ready to insert foot in mouth. Mick didn't know what had happened, but then again he didn't give anyone a chance to tell him.

He walked in and plonked himself in Pell's usual chair. Whoops! It was good manners to leave a dead pilot's seat vacant for a few days, a small memorial to an absent friend. Then he began to sound off: 'Let me tell you what I think of the war ... blah, blah. My opinion on aerial combat is ... blah, blah. You've just converted from FE8s to Nieuport 17s? Well, I've been training on ... blah, blah. What's your name? And how many Germans have you shot down?'

Mick Mannock during training with the RFC, 1916

Lieutenant Blaxland remembered:

*He seemed too cocky for his experience, which was nil.
New men usually took their time and listened to the
more experienced hands. Most men in his position, by
that I mean a man from his background and with his
lack of fighting experience, would have shut up and*

*earned their place in the mess. He seemed a boorish
know-all and we all felt the quicker he got amongst the
Huns the better.*

An Unusual Recruit

His new unit wouldn't have guessed, but Mannock's
brash manner was a mask to hide his nerves. He was 28
when he qualified as a pilot, much older than most new
recruits, who were little more than boys. His
background was different too – he was definitely not a
gentleman. He was probably born in Cork in Ireland (see
pages 112–13), hence the nickname 'Mick'. He had had a
working-class upbringing and had never set foot in a
posh public school.

Mick had seen the hard side of life. His father was a
soldier who had abandoned his mother, leaving her to
bring up the family in poverty. Mick had left school at 14
to start work in a grocer's shop before he eventually
became a telephone engineer. When war broke out in
Europe he was working to install a telephone system in
Turkey. It was an unfortunate place to be.

In 1915 Turkey joined the war on the German side
and Mick was interned. He almost starved to death in
the **internment camp** and carried a virulent hatred
of Germans from then on. It was German officers who
had asked the Turks to lock up British civilians and they
had done nothing to ease the dreadful conditions in
the camps.

After Mick had been repatriated (sent home in a deal brokered by the Americans) he joined the army and then requested a transfer to the RFC. He was bright, determined and quickly became a top student. One instructor wrote:

> He made his first solo flight in a Henri Farman with only a few hours' instruction. He seemed to master the rudiments of flying in his first hour in the air and from then on threw the machine about as he pleased.

Perhaps Mick could be forgiven, then, for thinking that he had qualities to offer 40 Squadron . . . if his fellow pilots would give him a second chance. But the coming days didn't improve matters.

A Windy Type

On his first patrols Mick seemed edgy. He'd make silly mistakes, wrongly setting his engine and dropping out of formation. His plane was the last to make a move and he seemed to lack energy and drive. The rumour went round that Mannock was a 'windy type' – a coward. And after his first combat experience, even Mick began to wonder if he had the nerve to be a fighter pilot.

On 13 April six planes from 40 Squadron crossed German lines, escorting RE8 reconnaissance planes. Soon they ran into heavy flak and the aircraft were bounced around the sky. As **Archie** exploded nearby Mick felt an awful dryness in his mouth and throat, and his stomach heaved. It was the sensation of cold unrelenting fear – and it didn't get any better during his next flights.

Fortune wasn't on Mick's side either. He was desperate to make his first kill and prove himself, but there always seemed to be a problem. On 1 May he was on patrol with his new flight commander, Captain Keen. The mission was risky, to photograph Douai aerodrome, the home of Manfred von Richthofen's Jasta. Mick wrote a vivid report in his diary:

We were attacked from above over Douai. I tried my gun going over German lines, only to find that it was jammed, so I went over with a revolver only. A Hun in a beautiful yellow and green 'bus' attacked me from behind. I could hear his machine-gun cracking away. I wheeled round on him and howled like a dervish (although of course he couldn't hear me) whereat he made off towards old Parry and attacked him, with me following for the moral effect! Another one (a brown speckled one) attacked a Sopwith, and Keen blew the pilot to pieces & the Hun went spinning down from 12,000 feet to earth. Unfortunately the Sopwith had been hit and went down too, and there was I a passenger, absolutely helpless, an easy prey to any of them … What is the good of it all?

Six days later Mick learned another lesson about the wastage of war. A flight (six aircraft) from 40 Squadron went on a balloon-busting operation. Led by Captain

Nixon, they flew barely 20 feet (6 m) above the ground for a hair-raising 5 miles (8 km) behind enemy lines. It was a lively trip. Again and again they breasted waves of ground fire until, balloons in sight, Nixon pointed each man to his target.

Nieuport 17 planes firing at balloons

Mick pulled down his goggles and arrowed his Nieuport towards the fat brown slug floating on the end of the cable. Pulling the trigger, he fired a burst of tracer and explosive bullets from point-blank range – and watched with delight as the balloon crumpled in flames. Mission accomplished, he put his head down below the cockpit **coaming** and headed for home.

When he landed Mick was euphoric.

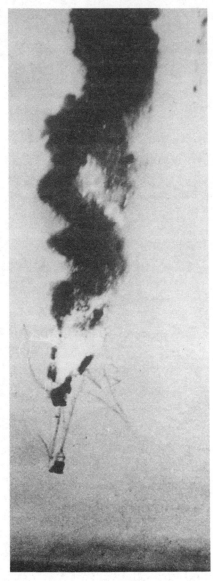

Two German balloons shot
down in France

I was the only one to return properly to the aerodrome, and made a perfect landing. We all got our objectives. My fuselage had bullet holes in it, one very near my head, and the wings were more or less riddled.

Then he heard the bad news. Just as the attack had gone in, Captain Nixon had scanned the horizon and spotted five Albatros DIIIs high above and ready to pounce. Knowing his unit was at a terrible disadvantage, he peeled off and climbed to meet the enemy. In a brief, wheeling dogfight Nixon was hopelessly outnumbered and shot down. His killer was Lothar von Richthofen, the brother of the Red Baron.

Practice Makes Perfect

While Mick was a competent, even skilful pilot, he wasn't a 'natural' like the Canadian Billy Bishop or England's favourite ace, Albert Ball. He had to work hard to improve and to overcome his own doubts. He carefully studied single-seater tactics and, crucially, developed his marksmanship.

Mick's spare hours were spent with his Nieuport pulled close to the butts while a bored mechanic yelled out the results of firing tests. Sitting on the edge of the cockpit, he would fine-tune the Lewis gun on the upper wing and align the sight on the front cowling. Again and again Mick would fire short bursts until he had the bullet pattern he wanted – a close group at a range of only 90–120 feet (28–37 m). After this came endless practice with the ground target, pulling out of screaming dives, guns blazing, only a few feet from impact. Now all he needed was that elusive change of luck. It finally came in June.

On 7 June Mick was escorting a formation of FE2b bombers to raid the town of Lille. Within seconds of their arrival over the target the bombers were jumped by a flight of Albatros scouts and Mick's flight of Nieuports went to the rescue. Picking out a German who was closing in on an FE, Mick attacked. That night he wrote in his diary:

My man gave me an easy mark. I was only 10 yards away from him – on top so I couldn't miss! A beautiful coloured insect he was – red, blue, green & yellow. I let him have 60 rounds at that range so there wasn't much left of him. I saw him going spinning and slipping down from 14,000.

Although Mick had hated Germans since his imprisonment, he was still shaken by the death of his enemies, as his next confirmed victory showed. After a period of leave in England he was soon back in action and eager to add to his score. On 12 July he set out to look for trouble over German lines and found it south-east of Lens.

He caught sight of two DFW two-seaters in the distance, turned away from them and climbed to 11,000 feet (3,400 m). Manoeuvring above and behind his victims, he dived on the one at the back and let loose a long burst of 90 rounds. The big machine flipped into a dive – out of control. Watching from 7,000 feet (2,150 m) Mick saw the DFW pile into the ground upside down behind British lines at Avion. When he landed he set out immediately for the crash site. It was to leave him with a lasting and troubled memory.

The DFW lay in a crumpled heap. The observer had been wounded and taken to hospital but the pilot had been killed. Mick was nauseated by the sight of the dead pilot and also a dead dog:

Mick Mannock firing at German planes

*I gathered a few souvenirs, though the infantry had the
first pick. The machine was completely smashed ... I
felt exactly like a murderer. The journey to the trenches
was rather nauseating ... This sort of thing ...
combined to upset me for days.*

Yet there was a hard and practical side to this grim
visit as well. Mick was still unsure about his shooting.
Was he hitting the target? How well were his bullets
grouping? The body of the pilot gave him the answer. In a
conversation with a friend he explained: 'It sickened me
but I had to see where my shots had gone. Do you know
there were three neat little bullet holes right here,'

pointing to the side of his head. 'I had to find out and this one down on our side was my only chance.'

Flight Command

As his victories mounted Mick came to be accepted and liked by most of the pilots of 40 Squadron. In August 1917 he was promoted to commander of A Flight and began the work that was to make him an outstanding leader. More than most RFC pilots he realized that the days of the lone-wolf ace were coming to an end. Teamwork was the key to success.

In combat Mick became less dashing and reckless, thinking through new tactics with endless planning meetings. He shared his ideas and built the confidence of his men. In the air A Flight practised formation attacks, stalking the enemy to look for a favourable position before pouncing. Crucially, new pilots were nursed until they had the skills to look after themselves. In five months Mick had grown from big-mouthed rookie to accomplished commander of the best flight in the squadron. It was only the start of an amazing career.

FIGHTING FACTS

Aces High

Pilots who shot down large numbers of enemy machines

became known as 'aces'. In a war where most men died anonymously, mown down by machine guns or searing artillery barrages, aces captured the public imagination. They seemed almost like knights of old, riding into a glamorous tournament in the air.

In Europe aces were treated like pop stars and became instant celebrities. Their pictures and autographs were collectors' items and they were mobbed by admiring crowds when they made public appearances.

Wartime Star – Germany

Max Immelman was Germany's first great ace. He was invited to dinner with the King of Bavaria. His Fokker was put on display in Berlin and he was inundated with fan mail.

Wartime Star – France

Georges Guynemer was awarded 15,000 francs by the Michelin tyre company, but in a typically grand gesture gave it away to a charity for the wounded.

Not at All British

In a stuffy British way, the RFC frowned on the idea of aces. General Haig, Commander in Chief of the British Army in France, wrote in 1917:

> I feel sure that officers of the RFC are proud of being anonymous like their comrades in other branches of the British Army.

Even Hugh Trenchard, Commander of the RFC, thought aces were overrated. He commented, 'A bomber raid on an enemy airfield can destroy more planes than all the aces in a week.' But he could see that aces had propaganda value and that their heroism could inspire other pilots.

The Top Ten British Empire Aces

An ace added to his score by shooting down or forcing down an enemy plane or airship. It still counted as a victory whether the enemy pilot was killed or not.

Name	Victories	Nationality
1. William Bishop	72	Canadian
2. Edward 'Mick' Mannock	61	British
3. Raymond Collishaw	60	Canadian
4. James McCudden	57	British
5. Anthony Beauchamp-Proctor	54	South African
6. Donald MacLaren	54	Canadian
7. William Barker	50	Canadian
8. Robert Little	47	Australian
9. George McElroy	47	Irish
10. Albert Ball	44	British

Mannock – Whose Ace, Ireland's or England's?

Mick's origins are a point of controversy. Although Edward Mannock was nicknamed 'Mick', his Irish connections may not have been that strong. His father,

Corporal Edward Mannock, was Scottish and his mother, Julia, was English, though possibly from Irish descent. Different accounts have him born in Brighton, Aldershot and Ballincollig, County Cork.

The Irish didn't push too strongly to claim Mick as their own because he was a Unionist. He believed Ireland should remain part of Britain at a time when the Irish struggle for independence was about to gain momentum. It was typical 'Mick', never afraid of an argument or an outspoken opinion.

Mick's Nightmare

Mick's problem with nerves never left him. Time and again he had to fight back his fears to take to the air. His worst nightmare was fire. On 4 September 1917 he shot down four aircraft. The last was a DFW two-seater that burst into flames and turned into a fireball. This kill stayed with him and hounded the dark parts of his mind. By 1918 he was suffering from exhaustion, caused by constant combat, and he began to take a sickening pleasure in seeing his victims on fire.

Mick was determined never to die that way. 'I'll put a bullet through my head if the machine catches fire . . . they'll never burn me,' he declared. But there is an old saying: If you want to make God laugh tell him your plans.

On 26 July 1918 Mick was shot down by ground fire. He had disobeyed one of his own rules – never follow the victim down. Horribly, his plane crashed in flames.

Lieutenant Donald Inglis was flying alongside Mick when he was shot down. He reported:

> *Mick fired at a two-seater. He must have got the observer, as the Hun stopped shooting. I fired and hit the Hun's petrol tank. Falling in behind Mick again, we did a couple of turns over the burning wreck and then made for home. We were fairly low, then I saw a flame come out of the side of his machine; it grew bigger and bigger. He went into a slow right-hand turn, about twice, and hit the ground in a burst of flame.*

Richthofen's Flying Circus
In the summer of 1917 the Germans refined their tactics again, grouping Jastas together into Jagdgeschwader (JG for short) or mobile fighter wings. Manfred von Richthofen was put in charge of JG No. 1 on 26 July. The unit was housed in tents and portable sheds that could

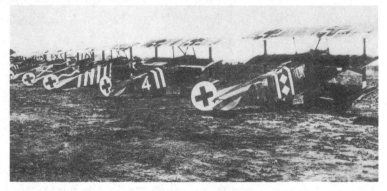

Richthofen's Flying Circus

be transported by train or lorry to any part of the battlefront where there was a crisis.

Pilots painted their machines in striking colours. One British pilot recalled fighting 'machines with green wings and yellow noses, silver wings and gold noses, red bodies with green wings, light blue bodies and red wings'. British airmen soon nicknamed JG 1 'The Flying Circus' because it moved around under canvas like a travelling circus and because of its garishly coloured aircraft. By 1918 there were four circuses flying over the Western Front, savaging the RFC whenever they took to the air.

The Red Baron

Of all the aces of World War 1, Baron Manfred von Richthofen, the Red Baron, was the most famous. He learned his flying skills on the Eastern Front against Russia and joined the fighting on the Western Front in 1916. He made his first kill on 17 September and his most notable two months later when he shot down the British ace Lanoe Hawker. Richthofen wrote:

*When he [Lanoe] had come down to about 300 feet
he tried to escape by flying in a zigzag course. I
followed him from an altitude of from 250 feet to 150,
firing all the time. The Englishman could not help falling
... shot through the head.*

Cool and steady in combat, Richtofen avoided

unnecessary risks and took his score up to 80, making his last two kills on 20 April 1918. The next day, in an unusually reckless attack, he chased his prey low over Allied lines on the Somme and was shot down by a combination of ground fire and the efforts of Canadian pilot Captain Roy Brown. Although badly wounded, Richthofen managed to land his Fokker triplane on a roadside, but died of his wounds. The Red Baron was buried by the RAF with full military honours.

Golden Rules for Staying Alive

Some aces stayed tight-lipped about their trade secrets. Their main aim was to build up their own scores. Others, like Mick Mannock, made a point of sharing their top fighting tips with young pilots. He realized that the only way to spike the circuses was through teamwork. By 1918 instructions to a rookie pilot would have gone something like this:

- Fly high and keep the sun behind you. **Beware the Hun in the sun!** If you start an attack, always finish it. Remember Mannock's tip: 'Gentlemen, always above; seldom on the same level; never underneath.'
- Try to attack from behind and stay there till you shoot the enemy down.
- If a Hun dives on you, don't try to evade him, turn and meet him head on.
- Never relax your concentration. Always know what is going on around you. Constantly scan the horizon,

looking for danger. What are those specks in the distance?

- Learn to use the clouds. If you fly just within the cloud fringe you will be invisible from below but still able to see what is going on underneath you.
- Stay in formation – killing is teamwork.
- If you are caught napping, get the hell out of it. He who fights and runs away, lives to fight another day.
- Think of your aircraft as a flying rifle and hold it steady. Yes, an ace like McCudden can hit a German at 1,200 feet (370 m), but most pilots can't – get in close.
- Spend your spare time at the shooting butts. Check the firing pattern of your guns and align them yourself for the range you want. Ira Jones likes to open fire at 225 feet (70 m), the Frenchman Fonck from 120–180 feet (37–56 m).
- Don't waste bullets – fire your machine guns in short bursts. The German Max Immelman claimed a kill with every 12 to 25 bullets. Load your own guns to avoid jams from defective bullets or belts.
- Know your aircraft and modify it to scrape out every bit of performance you can. McCudden **machined the cylinder heads** of his SE5a and pushed the ceiling 3,000 feet (923 m) over the official figure.

We Haven't Got a Hope in the Morning

To the tune of 'John Peel'

When you soar into the air in a Sopwith Scout,
And you're scrapping with a Hun and your guns cut out,
Well, you stuff down your nose till your plugs* fall out,
'Cos you haven't got a hope in the morning.

For a batman† woke me from my bed,
I'd had a thick night and a very sore head,
And I said to myself, to myself I said,
'Oh we haven't got a hope in the morning.'

So I went to the sheds and examined my gun,
then my engine I tried to run;
And the revs that it gave were a thousand and one;
'Cos you haven't got a hope in the morning.

For a batman woke me from my bed, etc.

We were escorting Twenty-two,
Hadn't a notion what to do,
So we shot down a Hun and an FE△ too,
'Cos you haven't got a hope in the morning.

* plugs: spark plugs in engine
† batman: servant
△ FE: British plane

118

SIXTY TO
ONE

BATTLE BRIEFING

By the end of 1917 the RFC had clawed back control of the air from the German Air Force. New planes came into service which more than matched the Albatros, notably the Sopwith Camel, the SE5A and the Bristol Fighter. The Camel, with its amazing aerobatic abilities and twin machine guns, soon became a firm favourite and logged more kills than any other aircraft in the RFC.

In 1918 the Germans planned a last desperate bid to win the war – before American troops arrived in large numbers – and air power was to be a key part of this. Under a plan called the Amerikaprogramm, aircraft production doubled to 2,000 planes a month, 24,000 new recruits were called up and the output of aviation fuel rose from 6,000 to 12,000 tons a month. By March the German Air Force had over 4,000 planes ready to support a great ground attack on the Western Front, most of them lined up against the RFC.

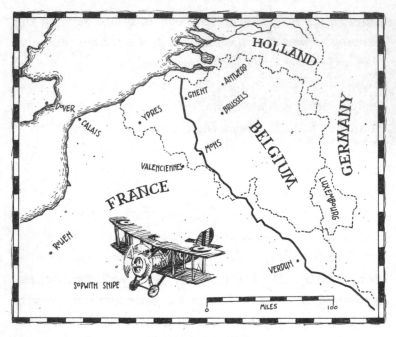

The Western Front, 1918

The assault – codenamed Operation Michael – was launched at 04:45 on 21 March with dreadful effect. Following close behind a huge bombardment, specially trained German storm troopers burst through the lines of the British Fifth Army. Four years of trench warfare came to a sudden end as the Allies were forced to make a fighting retreat. To add to the misery of the British troops, hundreds of enemy planes machine-gunned and bombed any pockets of resistance. These were the Schlastas (Battle Wings), specialized ground-attack formations, flying armoured two-seater fighters at heights of less than 325 feet (100 m).

Other units flew vital observation missions, keeping the generals informed of the progress of the ground troops, so that artillery fire could keep up with them.

For three long months the Germans pushed forward, almost reaching Amiens, and driving a wedge between the French and British armies. The French government, dreading the worst, made plans to abandon Paris. The turning point came in July. Now the German Army was exhausted and running short of supplies. It was time for the Allies, reinforced by America, to begin a series of devastating counter-attacks.

The German Air Force was better equipped, trained and supplied than ever before but the RFC, now renamed the RAF, hit back hard. British pilots fought massed air battles, grinding down the Germans and at the same time copying the tactics of the Schlastas to help their own infantry. Into this mayhem flew a skilled Canadian pilot fresh from the war in Italy – Major William Barker.

THE VISITING MAJOR

An Unwelcome Guest

The pilots of 210 Squadron were battle-hardened and weary. They had lived through the chaos of Operation Michael and suffered heavily in their dogfights with the multicoloured machines of the circuses. The last thing they needed was a Canadian tourist – however distinguished – foisted on them for a few days. OK, so he'd made his reputation fighting the Austrians on the Italian front. So what? Everyone knew Italy was a sideshow and the Austrians were pussycats compared to the Germans.

And to add insult to injury he'd grabbed one of the first Sopwith Snipes – the latest plane they were all eager to get their hands on. The rumour was it had a ceiling of 22,000 feet (96,770 m), with oxygen and an electrical heating system for the cockpit. So how come this visiting major was swanning about in one, while they had to carry on fighting with worn-out Camels! Unfair or what? The sooner he was gone the better!

The object of their scorn was Major William Barker, **DSO and Bar, MC and Two Bars**. But the pilots of

Four Sopwith Snipe Aircraft (No. 29 Squadron)

210 Squadron were more than a little unkind. Anyone who knew his record understood that Will Barker had nothing to prove.

Record of a Hero

Will was born in Dauphin, Manitoba, in 1893. He was a farm boy and a good shot with a rifle. Later, he was to show he could be every bit as accurate with a machine gun. He joined the Canadian Mounted Rifles in 1914 and spent a year in the trenches before transferring to the RFC in April 1916.

After starting as a mechanic, Will became an observer-gunner, flying in outdated BE2cs over the blood-soaked Somme. In September 1916 he and his pilot were sent out to photograph new German defences. Over enemy lines they were intercepted by two Albatros DIIs and their chances looked poor, but they inflicted so much damage on one machine that both broke off the attack. On the way back to base they were jumped again, this time fighting off four more German planes. Will was awarded his first Military Cross for this action.

In November 1916 Will was posted to England for training as a pilot. He'd gone solo after 55 minutes' flying time and gained his licence in January 1917. A month later he was back in France, this time in the cockpit of an RE8. During 'Bloody April' he flew daring observation missions, directing artillery fire on to German troops.

Major W. G. Barker beside his Sopwith Camel

On a mission in August 1917 Will was wounded by shrapnel in the side of his head and passed out from loss of blood. His observer saved the day by reviving him in time to land their plane safely.

In September Will was given a break and sent back to England to train new pilots. Here he got his first flight in a Sopwith Camel but soon grew bored with training. He wanted action. When his requests to be sent back to combat were ignored he **buzzed** Piccadilly Circus and RFC HQ. Back in France he served with 28 Squadron and ran his score up to six when he shot down two

Albatros fighters on the same day.

At the end of 1917 28 Squadron was transferred to the Italian front and over the next 10 months Will relentlessly chalked up kills – 46 enemy planes and nine balloons.

The Western Front Again

In September 1918 Will was ordered back to England, to take command of the fighter pilot training school at Hounslow, Middlesex. But once again he kicked against a job that took him away from the fighting. He argued with the top brass that he needed a short tour of duty back on the Western Front – to sharpen his skills against the latest German planes and tactics. It was clear the enemy was losing the war now, but the German Air Force remained a deadly opponent. How could he be a convincing leader if he hadn't faced the best the enemy had to offer? Reluctantly they gave in and allowed him a short, roving tour of the front. He could pick any plane and any squadron he wanted.

Will settled on 210 Squadron, based at Beugnâtre, France, because an old friend was there. The commanding officer was Major Cyril Leman, Will's pilot from the days when he was a rookie observer back in 1916. At least there would be one welcoming face for evening meals in the officers' mess.

It was just as well he had Leman to talk to. The other pilots never warmed to Will on his ten-day tour. And he did little to break the ice. He didn't drink, smoke or have much time for horseplay. He kept his own company on the ground and never flew in patrols in the air. He took off with the squadron but used the Snipe's high-altitude performance to hang hawk-like above them – hunting for targets. He was written off by the others as a bigheaded ace looking to boost his own score and reputation.

Will stayed with 210 Squadron for ten frustrating days, dogged by bad weather and bad luck. He barely saw a target, let alone got close enough for a kill. Then on 26 October the news came he had been dreading. The hunt was over. He was ordered to return the Snipe at once and report to Hounslow. Will was furious but had no choice ... except ... perhaps ...

VC Sunday

The next morning, Sunday, Will was up before dawn. The sky was brightening and the rain that had fallen all through the night had stopped. There was barely a cloud in sight. He took off for England but was determined to make one last detour – a short spin over German lines. Just in case.

Will had been in the air about 20 minutes when he noticed that a white German two-seater was doing a reconnaissance of the area. A Rumpler, he thought. It was well above him, 21,000 (6,460 m) feet or maybe even more. Jackpot. They were flying over the Mormal Forest, near Valenciennes. He glanced at his watch. It was 08:25.

Will felt a rush of excitement. If the war ended soon this might be his last chance to add to his score. Climbing steadily, he closed on the target. But he could tell this was not going to be an easy victory. The Germans were alert and well trained and they saw him coming. The Rumpler's pilot opened the throttle and manoeuvred the plane deftly so his observer could blast away at the 'Englishman'.

Wheeling and turning, the aircraft chased through the sky, each looking for an advantage. The German observer hit the Snipe several times but missed Will. Finally Will moved in from behind and a little below ... and at a range of 600 feet (185 m) fired a burst that killed or wounded the gunner. Now, with the enemy helpless, he fired burst after burst into the cockpit, engine and wings at point-blank range. The Rumpler broke apart and one airman parachuted to safety ... only one.

Will stared at his victim, watching the German's parachute blossom and the pieces fall. It was hypnotic, thrilling ...

It was stupid.

Will had lost his concentration.

Wham. He felt an explosion of pain as a bullet tore into his right thigh, smashing the bone and almost severing his leg. He had turned from hunter into prey.

In the long seconds Will had taken to enjoy his

victory, a Fokker DVII had sneaked up. Climbing steeply, the German had fired a long burst that nearly finished him. Whether through shock or instinct he threw the Snipe into a steep left bank and fell away. Turning tightly, both planes dropped thousands of feet before Will out-circled the Fokker and fired a burst into its fuel tank. It vanished in a wall of flame.

The Fokker DVII

But the Canadian's problems were just beginning! As he levelled out, Will found himself flying head on into the full strength of a circus – at least 60 DVIIIs in stepped-up formation from 8,000 feet (2,460 m). For a moment the Germans were stunned. Anxious heads scanned the horizon. Was this a trap? Where were the other English aircraft? For a few brief moments nothing happened. Then the most eerie air battle of the war began – sixty to one.

Will battles for his life as the Germans line up to attack!

Will, badly wounded and without a parachute, realized there was no chance of escape. 'If I'm going to die,' he thought, 'I'll take another Hun with me.' Wheeling on the tail of a Fokker, he fired two bursts and it fell away in a spin.

Satisfied the Snipe was alone, the other Germans peeled into flights of five and took turns to attack from different sides. One flight would wheel in from above and the next from below, so that no matter how Will looped or dived he was always a target. The Snipe was chewed up by gunfire – hit over 300 times – and Will wounded again in the left hip.

Fainting from blood loss, he plunged 6,000 feet (1,840 m) in a spin, until the rush of air revived him and he pulled out of his fall. But not out of trouble! This time he had levelled out in the lower tier of the circus and the German attacks began once more. In desperation he picked the nearest enemy plane and tried to ram it, firing as he neared. Just as he reached the Fokker it blew apart and fell away. But Will paid a price – he was hit in the left arm, smashing his elbow, and as he fainted again the Snipe plunged into another spin.

This probably saved his life. The crazy, gyrating fall made it difficult for the Fokkers to follow him down and get a clear bead on the target. Incredibly, as the Snipe neared the ground, Will woke again and saw a familiar sight on the horizon: observation balloons. Straightening out, he ran at low altitude towards British lines and crash-landed at 90 mph (144 kph) near 29 Kite Balloon Section.

The balloonists rushed to the wreckage and lifted the severely injured pilot free. The cockpit was drenched in blood and one of his legs seemed to be held on by a sinew alone. Will was rushed by motor tender to a field dressing station and then on to 8 General Hospital in Rouen. Doctors fought for hours to save his life and he was unconscious for 10 days.

On 11 November the Great War came to an end – and on 20 November Will Barker was awarded the Victoria Cross. The citation read:

> This combat, in which Major Barker destroyed four enemy machines (three of them in flames), brought his total success to fifty three enemy machines destroyed, and is a notable example of the exceptional bravery and disregard of danger which this very gallant officer has always displayed throughout his distinguished career.

FIGHTING FACTS

What Really Happened on 27 October?

The version of Will Barker's action you have just read is commonly accepted, but doubts have been raised by his latest biographer, Wayne Ralph.

- **Doubt 1** All the independent witnesses were on the ground and couldn't have seen what happened in detail.
- **Doubt 2** The combat report was written by Major Leman, the commanding officer of 210 Squadron, not Will himself. Will never gave a detailed account of the fight, except to say, 'I was severely injured and shot down.'
- **Doubt 3** Will's story became big news and an exaggerated legend. It's difficult to pick apart a fable

once it has gripped the public imagination.

- **The Big Doubt** The fuselage of Will's Snipe was shipped out to Canada in 1919 and was on display until 1996. It shows little evidence of being torn apart by enemy bullets. Wayne Ralph doubts that Will fought a full circus or shot down four enemy planes. Even so, he credits him with one kill and one probable kill and doesn't doubt his courage or that he tangled with a large formation of enemy planes. His book argues that William Barker should be remembered for his whole remarkable flying career, rather than just the VC episode.

Severe Wounds

Will never fully recovered from his wounds, though he lived on till 1930 and flew again. He had been hit by high velocity, 7.92-mm bullets travelling at more than 2,500 feet (770 m) per second. These tumble in the air, increasing the damage when they hit a body. The shock wave generated in front of each bullet and the **cavitation** behind force human tissue to stretch and recoil some distance from the wound track. Angry Allied pilots wrongly accused the Germans of using explosive bullets.

Courageous Camel

Will shot down most of his kills flying the same plane in Italy – a Sopwith Camel B6313. Even when his squadron all changed to the excellent Bristol FE2, Will hung on to his Camel. It logged more than 379 hours of flight time and became the single most successful aircraft in the war. B6313 was retired from service and dismantled on 2 October 1918.

Parachute Problems

Will Barker couldn't escape by parachute after he was injured on 27 October – *because he didn't have one!* Yet as early as the 1880s parachutes had been shown to work, with circus showmen using them jumping from balloons at a great height and landing safely. By 1917, French, German and US pilots were all equipped with 'chutes. Even British balloonists had them – but not the RFC.

R. E. Calthorpe, a retired British engineer, had developed a compact parachute nicknamed 'the Guardian Angel' before the war. He told the RFC about his invention and successful tests were carried out at the Royal Aircraft Factory at Farnborough. Despite good results, Sir David Henderson, Commander of the Royal Flying Corps, refused to issue them. Two main arguments were used against them, one practical and one moral:

- Even the Guardian Angel was too bulky and heavy, and therefore likely to affect the performance of an aircraft.
- Nothing should be done to 'impair the fighting spirit of pilots and cause them to abandon machines which might otherwise be capable of returning to base for repair'.

Aces like Mick Mannock were driven wild by the

Kite balloon observers preparing to descend by parachute

arrogant stupidity of the 'top brass' . . . and hundreds of pilots died needlessly.

Lessons Forgotten

The RFC grew from a tiny band of pilots into the finest air force on the Allied side, with over 22,000 aircraft in service by 1918. No longer underpowered string bags fit only for watching armies on the ground, planes had become fast, reliable and deadly. And the pace of change did not slacken. By the middle of World War II, barely 25 years later, aircraft were capable of devastating enemy cities and grinding armies to a halt. Crucially, the atomic bombs that brought that war to an end were dropped from the air.

Favourite Mess Song of the Lafayette Escadrille, a Unit of American Pilots Flying with the French Air Force

We meet 'neath the sounding rafters,
The walls all around us are bare;
They echo the peals of laughter;
It seems that all the dead are there.

So stand by your glasses steady,
This world is a world of lies.
Here's a toast to the dead already;
Hurrah for the next man who dies.

Cut off from the land that bore us,
Betrayed by the land that we find,
The good men have gone before us,
And only the dull are left behind,

So stand by your glasses steady,
The world is a web of lies.
Then here's to the dead already,
And hurrah for the next man who dies.

RFC LINGO

ace a pilot with a large number of kills. The highest-scoring British ace was Edward Mannock with 73.

Archie anti-aircraft fire. The explanation is complicated! A London show in 1914 had a song in which a young lady stopped her boyfriend from smooching with the catchphrase 'Not now, Archie.' One pilot used to yell this every time his plane came under fire . . . and pretty soon it caught on.

Beware the Hun in the sun! look out for enemy planes attacking out of the sun. This made them hard to spot. Pilots needed rubber necks.

Boche nickname for a German

buzzed flew very low over

ceiling the highest a plane can reach.

CO commanding officer.

dogfight a shoot-out in the air.

Hun unsavoury nickname for a German, after the barbaric Huns of history.

joystick control lever that could be operated with one hand.

pusher aircraft with rear-mounted engine and propeller.

sausages observational balloons with elongated gasbags.

scout a fast single-seater plane, originally designed for quick reconnaissance flights. These became the aircraft sent up to intercept enemy machines. By 1918 'scout' had come to mean the same as 'fighter' today.

scrambled ordered to get into the plane.

tractor aircraft with front-mounted engine and propeller.

witches' water gasoline. It was given the nickname because many pilots burnt to death when their fuel ignited.

GLOSSARY

butts targets

cavitation low pressure

coaming raised edging to keep the wind out

Commandered taken from their civilian owners

Communist Revolution revolution to overthrow the Russian monarch, the Tsar, and to improve the lives of the people.

conscripts soldiers who are ordered to join the army by the government

cowling engine cover

cut daisies to skim very low to the ground.

drum a round magazine of bullets for quick loading into a machine gun

DSO and Bar, MC and Two Bars Will Barker had an impressive array of medals, the Distinguished Service Order and the Military Cross. A bar is a strip of silver below the clasp of a medal, to show the wearer has been recognized for bravery again.

elevators control surface used to climb or dive in an aircraft or airship

fuselage body of a plane

internment camp prison camp for enemy civilians

jam on full aileron and rudder set the controls to turn the plane over

a kill shooting down or forcing an enemy plane to land, not necessarily killing the enemy crew

Lewis gun a light, reliable machine gun

machined the cylinder heads modified the engine to increase the power

manoeuvres war-training exercises

put on rudder turned sharply

Tommies German nickname for British soldiers

ACKNOWLEDGEMENTS

Thanks to George Tones, for checking the technical spec. on the aircraft.

W. B. Yeats: 'An Irish Airman Foresees His Death' from *Collected Poems* by W. B. Yeats, by permission of A. P. Watt Ltd on behalf of Michael B. Yeats.

Picture Credits
IWM: p.12 HU71314 p.14 Q54985 p.18 Q66961 p.34 Q33781 p.36 Q67465 p.46 Q69222 p.56 Q58460 p.59 Q66935 p.73 Q80142 p.80 Q63785 p.86 HU71312 p.101 Q73408 p.114 Q58034 p.122 Q69782 p.124 Q27508 p.128 Q67207 p.134 Q27506

p.54 © Punch Ltd.